Y0-BUB-464

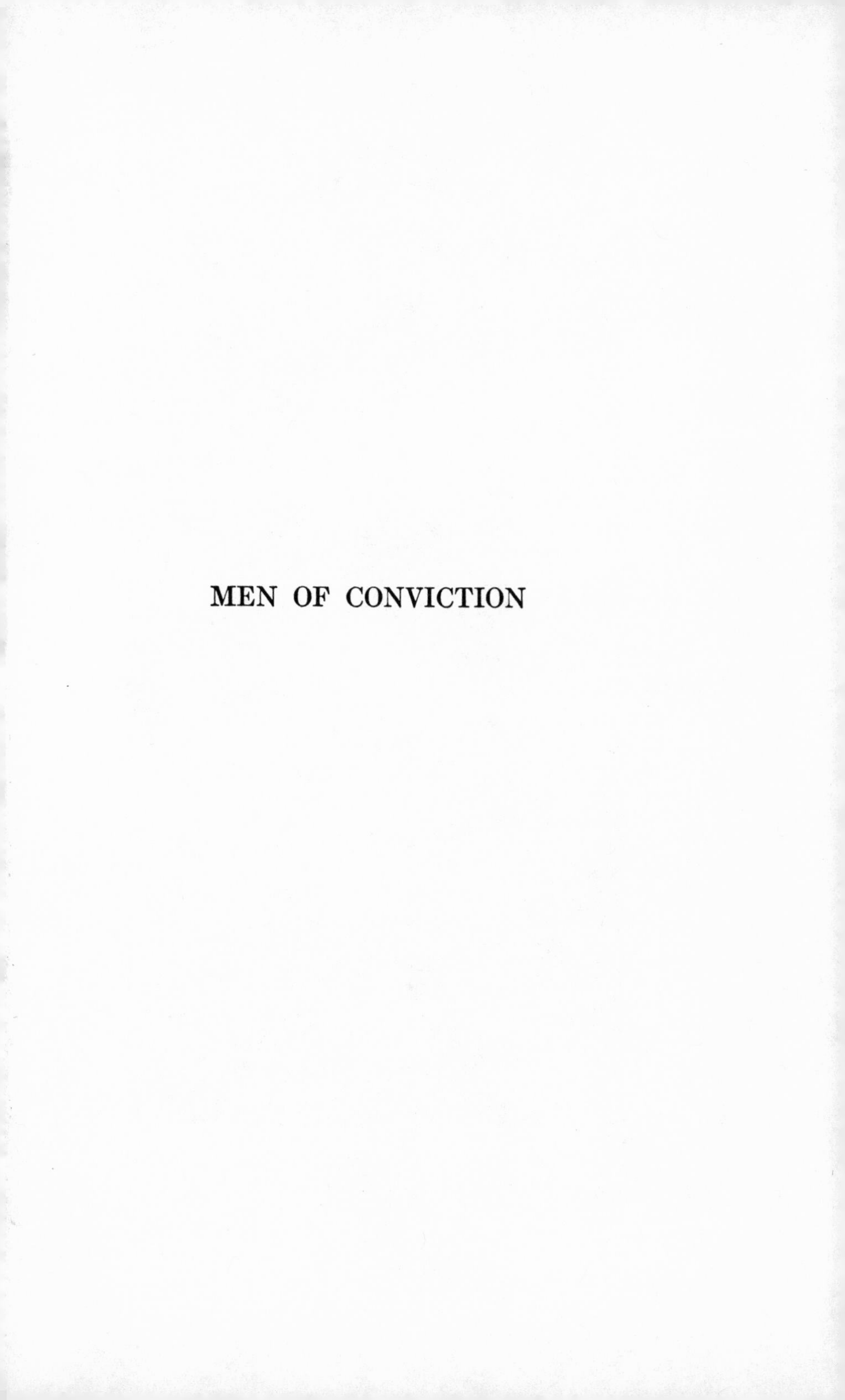

MEN OF CONVICTION

*Photo, Archives Photographiques d'Art et d'Histoire, Paris.*

ST. FRANCIS RECEIVING THE STIGMATA

From the painting by Giotto in the Louvre

# MEN OF CONVICTION

BY

HENRY BRADFORD WASHBURN

*Essay Index Reprint Series*

BOOKS FOR LIBRARIES PRESS
FREEPORT, NEW YORK

Reprinted 1971 by arrangement with
Charles Scribner's Sons

INTERNATIONAL STANDARD BOOK NUMBER:
0-8369-2081-3

LIBRARY OF CONGRESS CATALOG CARD NUMBER:
74-134152

PRINTED IN THE UNITED STATES OF AMERICA

TO MY WIFE

# PREFACE

THE six biographical sketches which follow are the Bohlen Lectures for 1931. Although the lectures were given altogether without notes, they were written in full and put into the form of a book before the time of delivery. As one who reads the first chapter will see, the sketches were written at various times and in various places, time and place being largely determined by my ability to get near the haunts of the man whose thought and conduct I was studying. Much of the material I have used on other occasions and in other ways. The old material and the new are now gathered together and made a unit because of their meaning in my own religious experience. I am grateful to the editors of *The Anglican Theological Review* for permission again to publish the chapter on Ignatius Loyola, the only portion of the book that has appeared in public print, and to Dean Green of the Alexandria Theological Seminary and to the Central Church of Worcester, Massachusetts, for permission to reprint such portions as have appeared, respectively, in the Reineker and Merriman Lectures. I want also to thank my colleague, The Rev. Professor William

H. P. Hatch of The Episcopal Theological School, and Professor Kenneth J. Conant of Harvard University for giving me the use of illustrations in their possession.

H. B. W.

THE EPISCOPAL THEOLOGICAL SCHOOL,
CAMBRIDGE, MASSACHUSETTS,
January, 1931.

## CONTENTS

# ILLUSTRATIONS

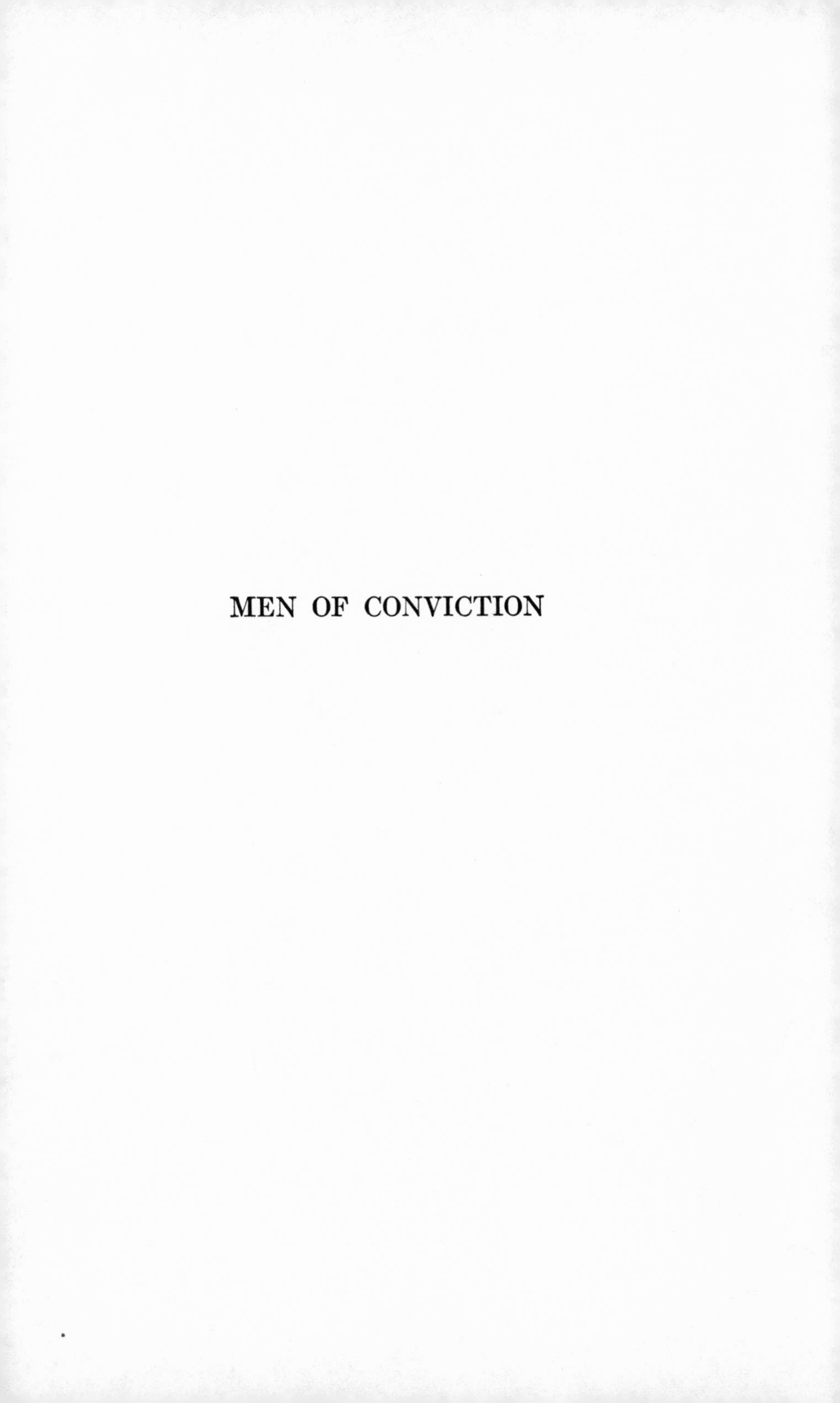

MEN OF CONVICTION

# CHAPTER I

## AUTOBIOGRAPHIC

SHORTLY after the beginning of my ministry I remember saying to Dr. Vinton, of Worcester, that some day the doctrine of the Trinity ought to be restated in terms of religious experience. He answered, "Why don't you do it yourself?" It is needless to say that up to the present moment I have never done it, nor have I thought myself qualified to do it in the way that at the time I thought it ought to be done. But the strong conviction that it should be done has never left me, and the underlying general principle that doctrine, in so far as it is valuable, is nothing more or less than an attempt to explain religious experience, has dominated all my thought and all my teaching.

Between fifteen and twenty years ago, in consequence of such an overmastering idea, I noticed that a change was almost unconsciously taking place in my methods of teaching. Theretofore my interest had been in events, in movements, in institutions, in doctrines. Thereafter it shifted gradually to a curiosity about the man or the men in whose life the event had taken place, or whose energy had brought the event to pass, to a desire intimately to know those whose inspiration and enthusiasm had brought the institution into existence, and whose contagious conviction had given it momentum. I found myself forgetting Christianity and thinking about Christ; not caring whether the fifteenth chapter of First Corinthians formed an unassailable argument for immortality, but asking myself what it meant to St. Paul; passing from the persecution to the persecutors and the persecuted; regarding the doctrine of the Trinity as purely secondary and insufficient and the convictions of Athanasius as primary and utterly satisfying; appraising the doctrine of The Two Natures as merely an outward sign of what individuals like Cyril of Alexandria thought of Christ and of what the entire unnamed Christian population of the West, as they were represented by Leo I, were convinced that Christ must be. And passing in such a way from the impersonal to the personal, I found myself giving my classes the alternative of reading general Church histories or reading religious biography. Fully persuaded that religious experience is the stuff out of which institutions and doctrines are made, that the experience is eternal while the expression of it is temporal, I have given it the first place in the students' lives and in my own, and, in consequence, for me at least, the study of the dead past has become a very vital and contemporary affair.

So much for the beginning of things. Now for certain of the results as I perceive them present in my own heart and mind. Although I could single out twenty or more men to whose religious experience I have given rather special and close study, and although I might name as many more in whom I find a dramatic presentation of certain aspects of moral, ecclesiastical or religious truth, I shall confine myself to six who have been the object of my most recent study, to each one of whom I owe a debt, and every one of whom illustrates, in my own religious experience at any rate, the practical value of religious biography. When grouped together they are a rather strange sextette. But for possibly just this reason all the more to my purpose, for our religious demands, while grouped together, are a singular and apparently unrelated collection of needs, and our religious conclusions the consequence of an accumulation of causes, some of which seem totally unrelated to one another.

My men are Athanasius, Benedict, Hildebrand, St. Francis, Ignatius Loyola and Pius IX. You will notice that not one of them is a Protestant Episcopalian, not even Athanasius! You will also notice that Athanasius is the only one to whose contribution to theological thought most Christians would subscribe, and that St. Francis is the only other who has exercised any direct and profound religious effect upon us in these later days. Benedict is, popularly speaking, only an interesting and forceful person who in about the year 530 wrote a monastic rule and founded an order, a bit of ecclesiastical archæology! Hildebrand is a visionary who, somewhat more than five hundred years later, made the startling claim that the Church was superior to the State—well enough for those days, we say, rather absurd in our own! Ignatius Loyola is a man who saw visions; he is the founder of the Order of Jesuits. Enthusiasm of his kind is still somewhat suspect, and the reputation of the Jesuits of the middle seventeenth century has besmirched even Ignatius himself! Pius IX is almost a joke. How could the man who said, "La tradizione son' Io," "I am Tradition," or, to turn a favorite expression of Louis XIV, "L'Eglise c'est moi," and the man who fought to the last trench against Italian national unity, be other than a pitiable survival of mediævalism, this expression being an indication of complete rejection? These four of my sextette are, on the whole, so far as they concern us, exotic. Practically, they represent types of religious experience which we imagine ourselves to have outgrown or which for one reason or another we have abandoned. It is little help to say that before the year 1500 we were of their Church or they of ours. So far as we are conscious of influences from any of them, Athanasius and St. Francis alone have survived. They alone have a message for the present which all of us at least in a measure confess.

And yet at the heart of the very reasons for the undervaluation of two of these and the widespread modern neglect of the other four, I find my reason for giving them thorough attention and for assuming that they stand for something of vital moment. I take it for granted that those who seemed to do a work essential to their own day expressed in the doing of it a principle of permanent, of undying, value. Benedict in writing his rule and in directing his monks can be passed by only at the cost of modern and immediate religious truth. Pius IX in ingenuously confessing that before 1870 he believed in Infallibility and after 1870 he was fully persuaded of it, and in saying to the ambassadors on the morning of the fateful September 20, "Gentlemen, I am now the prisoner of King Victor Emmanuel," may be laughed at only at our religious and political cost. With these two illustrations my fundamental principle should be at once apparent. It is not that the value of religious experience should be appraised in terms of sympathy and of intellectual assent to the details of their contemporary or long distant expression. It is rather that it should be weighed by the less palpable balances of earnestness, sincerity, high-mindedness, unselfishness and God-consciousness. To face the logic of this principle calls not only for imagination, but for courage, possibly for recklessness, uncommon to the Protestant, for even an inquisitor may be earnest, sincere, high-minded, unselfish and God-conscious. Cranmer and Bloody Mary alike shared these qualities. So did Athanasius and Julian the Apostate.

My task, therefore, is to find the permanent in the transitory, the perfect in the imperfect, even the good in the bad. It is to call to my service and to regard as essential even those things the manifestation of which stirs in me no response or sympathy, and even those things the manifestation of which seems to me of questionable value. That is the extreme statement of the case; it is the declaration that I am aware of the difficulties into which loyalty to the principle might lead me. The test cases with which I am now concerned will strain the principle, but not, I hope, to the breaking-point.

The doctrines which we call the Trinity, The Two Natures and The Two Wills, in other words the doctrines which affirm that our Lord is both perfectly human and perfectly divine, have always been a part of my religious belief. I cannot remember the time when I did not accept them. They have always seemed to me to be fundamentally reasonable. But that is where they have begun and ended. They have been fundamentally reasonable and nothing more. They have been admirable theory, and as such they have never touched my soul. In fact as long as I held these doctrines as theory I felt that I was rather on the defensive both in lecturing about them and in discussing them. They were in the realm of interesting and vulnerable philosophy rather than in that of warm and vivid religious experience.

But quietly, imperceptibly, a change has taken place; with the shifting of my method of approach the theory has passed into feeling, the reasonableness has become assurance. Now I am ready to try to hold my own in their favor. I account for this change altogether from the fact that I have, through my study of religious experience, begun at the other end. It is almost literally true to say that Athanasius has persuaded me, and this not so much from anything he said as from the cumulative effect of the feeling, conduct and thought of his long life.

If you will survey the life of Athanasius from early manhood to the day of his death you will be struck with the fact that he seems to have had a religious experience of which his whole career is an expression. The beliefs with which he appears on the stage of history are the same as those he held when he left it. His task was to impart it to people. The content of the experience was that the Jesus of history and the immanent Christ could not be rightly thought of except in terms of the divine. The facts of the daily life of Jesus—what He said, what He did and what He was—that perfect adjustment through love to the men and the world of his day—were to Athanasius indisputably divine. The Persuasions, if I may call them such, of the immanent Christ, which were of the same character as the earthly influence of Jesus, were essentially those of God. This personal aspect of the life of Athanasius has taken hold of me; it has won me. Alone it might have conquered me for the doctrines. But when I find that his convictions, by their sheer contagion and by their representative character, gradually became, through fifty years of testing in life and thought, the expressed mind of the Church, I submit to him entirely. I am an Athanasian. And I use his terms, not because they will be forever sufficient to express my idea of Christ, but because up to the present I can find no better. His religious experience has made the consubstantiality of Christ a very personal matter.

To pass from Athanasius to Benedict is to make an abrupt transition. It takes one into a totally different sphere of thought, but from the point of view of historical imagination and religious sympathy a sphere that is none the less important and personal. When I was a student in college and in the seminary, and during practically all my parochial ministry and the first years of my teaching, monks and monasticism were, in so far as they were of any interest, a matter of purely archæological moment. They were a stage through which Christianity had passed, possibly a stage which might have been avoided had our Lord been better understood. And their survival at present, whether in Romanism or Anglicanism, seemed to me to be in the same class with many of the useless biological survivals. But, having an instinctive knowledge that there was something wrong in this way of thinking, that possibly it implied that God was a little more wasteful in His processes than He really is, I turned to the life of one of the greatest of all the monks, Benedict, the father of the many rules of the West. And, although my course of study was not arranged in this order, I came to another point of view along the following path—I read all I could lay hold of on Benedict the man, what he said about himself, his rule, what others said of him, particularly Gregory the Great, his disciple and biographer, and I visited in one way or another many of the spots familiarly associated with his name. From Perugia I looked across thirty miles of country at the Sibellini, the snow-capped Apennines at the foot of which he was born. I crossed the Tiber by the Isola Tiberina and stood near the site of his boyhood home. I drove out beyond Tivoli to Subiaco, the wild and picturesque region where Benedict lived as a hermit and later as an abbot, and there I ate with the monks in their refectory. I went to Monte Cassino—the commanding headland on the southernmost point of which he built his monastery and where he himself became the wise rule of his fellow-monks. All this to make the man real to me! And I gathered together the results of my wanderings among books and valleys and hills in the Vatican Library—only a few hundred yards away from the site of his father's house.

And to what purpose? Not only has Benedict become to me a real and vivid personality, but the monastic mood and the monastic point of view have become factors of possibly permanent importance within my own life and that of the Christian Church. Benedict stood for seclusion, for meditation, for prayer and for manual labor. He stood for the principle that in order to save society some of its members must leave it, that in order that great throngs of men may pray a little a few men must pray much, and that contact with the very soil itself refines and keeps healthy the spiritual life. This is Benedict's contribution; it has much of eloquent emphasis. Mastered by

Benedict wherever in history I run across an example of high-minded monasticism, be it of the hermit or the community sort, and wherever in the Romanism or Anglicanism of to-day I discover men of this type who are living unselfishly and honestly, with supreme peace of mind, with some sign that they have been with Jesus, I say that in some way they are doing a work essential to themselves and necessary to the kingdom of God. My former feeling of opposition, my thought that they are a mere survival, has completely vanished. Benedict has given me eyes to see their permanent value. But by Benedict I mean the man whose monastic methods were a means for making real the presence and companionship of God, and conversely whose consciousness of the presence of God found its relief and expression in the monastic method. There is something in the monastic method of permanent meaning to the Christian Church. The experience of a good man, a religious genius, makes this assertion abundantly clear to me.

I am in Hildebrand's debt almost *because* of my congenital Puritanical hostility to a man of his type, *because* of my long-cherished opposition to the leaders of movements of strong Papal flavor, and *because* of my interest in those men, whether in England or on the Continent, whose influence paved the way for the Reformation and for English ecclesiastical independence. Instinctively I had long known that there was something not only narrow-minded, but unsound historically, in this point of view. My progress toward my present feeling may be described by a phrase that originally was used to illustrate what I trust may seem the opposite of my present purpose. Hildebrand I first "endured, then pitied, then embraced." What took place to work the change? On carefully examining Hildebrand's life I could not discover the guile I expected to find in it. I could come across no final evidence of selfishness. I could not get materials for a case to prove conclusively that he loved rule for the sake of ruling, that he strove for the supremacy of Rome for the sake of Roman supremacy, that he fought to place the Church supreme over the State for the prestige it might give him either personally or as the Head of the Church. Instead of all this I found myself yielding to the influence, or to the character, shall I say, of a straightforward and a self-forgetful person—a man who fought for celibacy and practised it; a man who would completely separate Church and State and whose conduct for fifty years harmonized with his theory; a man who would purify the morals of the clergy and whose own private life was spotless; a man who thought that religion should direct politics, to whom the Church was religion, and therefore a man who believed that in certain affairs of international moment the Church should be superior to the State, and died rather than surrender even some of the less important aspects of his claim. Many years ago I visited Hildebrand's grave at Salerno. Four years ago I thought of him as I passed near Canossa and as I wandered about his last refuge, the castle of St. Angelo. I could not, and I cannot, bring myself to believe that there is nothing but waste in such a life and in the lives of those who held his point of view. I must believe that at the heart of his consecration there is an ideal which many of the antipapally inclined fail to perceive—an ideal most practically necessary in his day (although not necessarily in the form in which he conceived it) and an ideal at the heart of which lies a truth essential to the exaggerated nationalism of the present day. My sympathies as to detail may lie with his enemies, but Hildebrand himself in his abandonment to the ideals of personal and international righteousness has made my understanding of mediæval history and my imagination as to the modern need of certain mediæval principles vastly more vivid. His life revealed an attitude toward Society which has made me dream of an essentially Christian League of Nations.

Almost every one owes some kind of a debt to St. Francis. My own debt to him is very heavy.

He has taught me to understand our Lord more clearly and personally than I had thought possible. He has done so in three ways. By doing miracles he has made the miracle comprehensible; by acting in an apparently superhuman way he has opened up a comprehension of the powers of human nature of which I had hardly dreamed; by daily walking with God he has made God-companionship pass from the realm of theory to that of fact.

Sabatier's book[1] of course it was that drew me strongly to St. Francis. However, since reading that and other "lives" I have read a little more widely and deeply in the Franciscan legends and in contemporary chronicles; I have followed this method and accompanied it by visiting nearly all the places associated with Francis' life—the most appealing of all being the font in which he was baptized and the mount on which he received the stigmata. Walking over the Umbrian Plain, sitting on the terrace at Perugia and letting my eyes rest on the little city of Assisi as it nestles against the steep side of Subasio, wandering into the glen of the Carceri—all of this has made Francis very real to me. Real, however, not merely as an historic character, of whom the records amply testify, but as a man who had broken through the superficial crust of his nature, as none in the West but

[1]Paul Sabatier, *Life of St. Francis of Assisi.*

Christ has done to so great a degree, and had shown what was in man. At the heart of his nature was an unselfish love of overwhelming vividness and creative energy. His mind was governed by the point of view of Christ and God. He looked at nature and human nature through his own eyes, but none the less through those of Christ and God—and at their worst nature and human nature were, because of the eyes that beheld them, very good. At the heart of his own being he had discovered himself, but he had also discovered Christ and God. With this community of being he was, like Christ and God, a creator. Things and men moved at his touch and word. This conclusion I cannot resist, although I have kicked against these pricks for years. And in consequence certain hitherto inscrutable, incomprehensible things have become clear. Granted pure unselfishness and single-hearted devotion and love —the supreme loss of one's self in another—and one immediately is confronted with the power by which the whole creation moves. Francis releases his own deep nature (he had power to release it and that power may be the only point at which he differs from us and resembles Christ) and it cures a leper; it goes out in affection toward birds and animals, and they yield to its persuasive loveliness; it gathers around the hard, the fearful and the suffering experience of Christ, and it creates in hands and feet and side the marks of the Lord.

I am fully aware that I ought to have come to understand Francis through Christ, but as a matter of fact I have come to understand Christ through Francis. I feel as if I had laid hold on the inner nature of Christ as a miracle-worker, and of Christ the creator—the Lord of birds and beasts and men, and the manifestation of the God-head bodily. And I feel also that I understand, in a small measure, the literal power of the teaching of our Lord. With Francis' example as my warrant, I am, I think, master of what Jesus meant when he said "But greater things than these shall ye do" and when he conditioned the coming of the kingdom of God on loving those that hate us and blessing those that persecute us. I am persuaded that these precepts work, and that men cannot resist essential goodness. I am, through him, persuaded that we are not ourselves until we are Christ's, that Christ is not Himself unless He is God's, and that God is not Himself until He is we. This is a heavy debt to confess to anyone. But I gladly say that Francis has brought me near to Christ and God and that he has directed me toward my own truer and essential self.

Ignatius Loyola has taught me that God speaks to each of us in a language each can understand, and that we communicate with Him in terms that are peculiarly sensitive to the expression of our natures. In other words he has done much, if not all, to encourage me not to divide types of religious experience and worship into groups of right and wrong, but rather to look upon all expressions of association with God, provided they are sincere, and provided they issue in religious comfort and in kindly action, as equally essential. If not altogether drawn to this point of view by Ignatius, I have at least been finally persuaded by him of its validity. In consequence I am no longer a believer in my own religious practices except for myself and those who are like-minded. I am no longer interested in programmes for the propagation of certain points of view and the suppression of others on the ground of their objective truth or falsehood. My only interest lies in the value of such beliefs to varying kinds of people—people who seem to me honest and unselfish and friends of God. Neither the memorial view of the Lord's Supper, nor the theory of the Real Presence, nor the doctrine of Transubstantiation means anything to me as such, apart from the people who hold and are helped by any one of them. Each has an infinite meaning to me when it is the apparent means by which a soul communes with God. More than this! Each is equally the God-chosen as well as the man-chosen medium of communion.

Ignatius would hardly thank me for acknowledging my indebtedness to him for this. For he himself held no such views. But courtesy compels me to do so, for he has forced me to acknowledge the validity of the spiritual experience which, before my study of him, was either unreal or absurd. When I hear him say that he stood before the altar and with the eye of the spirit saw the bread and wine change into body and blood, and when I see him pass out from such an experience and with supreme calmness and common sense superintend the education and the charities of the Order of Jesuits, I am compelled to respect an experience that may be no greater and no truer than the experiences of Zwingli and Cranmer, but if goodness and God-consciousness are any warrant of validity, at least as great and true. For my present purposes it makes no difference to me whether the experience was subjective or objective. My present conviction is that the language of Ignatius means something real in his relationship with God—something at least subjectively objective, if I may coin a phrase that may indicate a very tenuous objectivity—and that however preposterous it may seem to me it is a necessary method of communication between Ignatius and God—their mutual language.

Pius IX has challenged my historical imagination and my religious sympathies more vigorously than any other of my sextette. Until very recently he has stood in my estimation for practically everything religious and ecclesiastical and political with which I do not agree. Within a very few years I have used him as an illustration of all that one should not hold in regard to Church and State. Possibly because I stand at the very antipodes from him he has excited my interest and attention and piqued my curiosity. I will not put it so strongly as to say that the fool that came to scoff remained to pray, but I will say that some subtle and indefinable attraction has drawn me to him and that I have thought it worth while to take him seriously and to ascertain the significance of such a strange ecclesiastical paradox and political anomaly. Naturally I mean Pius IX not merely as an individual, but also as representative of the throng whose convictions he expressed.

In my effort to understand him better I not only have carefully reviewed the history of the movements toward Italian Independence and the declaration of the doctrine of Infallibility, but I have wandered about the city of Rome with Pius in mind; I have sought out and studied paintings that have the events of his pontificate as their subjects; and I have spent many hours writing and thinking of him in the library of the English College at Rome—a place the atmosphere of which was congenial to such an occupation, where

Manning lived as he worked day and night for the doctrine of Infallibility. And I have sauntered through the rooms and halls and quadrangles of the Vatican with Pius in mind.

Such a method has not blinded me to his startling and dramatic limitations, nor has it changed in the slightest my former opinion in regard to the double event of 1870. Pius was a sweet-natured man, of charming manners, of winning personality, of strong pastoral instinct and of vivid religious conviction. But his religious imagination was meagre and his ecclesiastical advisers left much to be desired. He began his rule with many sound ideas in regard to social and political reform and throughout his long pontificate he displayed a certain amount of political sagacity (to approve of Mussolini is unwittingly to compliment Pius IX). But the universal developing self-consciousness of nations has shown him to be hopelessly in the wrong in his tenacious hold on Rome.

And yet the supreme and representative satisfaction he showed when declared infallible in pronouncing on matters of faith and morals (Manning's persistence and vigor in working for the doctrine and his joy in its definition are sufficient evidence that the Pope's peace was not solely personal) leads me to look beyond the superficial character of the doctrine itself to the truth that may lie within, for me at least, its somewhat unattractive exterior. I find within it a feeling toward a truth fundamental to the individual and society—that somewhere, even now, we must look for the union of the divine and the human in the individual, that there is nothing antecedently absurd in the notion that a man may express the truth, and that this may be possible when the individual in question speaks for the group. My quarrel with the Infallibilists is not with the doctrine of Infallibility, but rather with their idea of truth.

Also within the Pope's dogged and reactionary and unreasonable fight to hold the temporal power I see truth that may always be found in tragedy. Superficially I see the belated, the threadbare, the fully discarded theory that the Church should wield political power. But fundamentally the Pope, without knowing it, was insisting that the Capital and Christianity may not be separated; that the internationalism of religion should not be jeopardized by the loss of the one city the nature of which for centuries had been imperial; that nationality and internationality must be controlled by religion. Discarding the form of his faith and remembering only the spirit within it I am looking for its better incarnation.

Such are some of the practical consequences of my study of religious biography. In detail I am in debt to certain men of the past. Their characters and their contributions to religion have greatly widened and deepened my comprehension of religion.

But for me these men and many others have greatly enriched the meaning of the Christian centuries. Whereas once I looked upon certain of them as men of value and upon others as men who quite as well might not have been born, I now approach men of all kinds, provided they led lives of unselfishness and of God-consciousness, expecting that they have something to give me. I am seldom disappointed. And whenever disappointment is my lot it is probably due to my poverty-stricken imagination as to the ways of God rather than to the nature of the religious experience in question. Whereas at one time, not many years ago, those movements in history and those men were of vital moment to me if they prepared the way directly or indirectly for those aspects of the Church and the Faith to which I could give my detailed allegiance, now there is hardly a movement or a man in the last two thousand years from which and from whom I may not expect to learn some positive truth.

More than this! Continuous thinking about these and other men has, in a very real sense, made them my contemporaries—almost contemporaries in time, literally contemporaries so far as their religious experience is concerned. The cross-section of time which we call the Christian era is so brief a portion of recorded history that its first year and its last seem uncomfortably close together when we think of the work that has been compressed between them. Fifty generations of septuagenarians might not only span the space, but they might overlap one another so generously that they might easily transmit the tradition. The convictions which the leaders of Christian thought and experience have represented are vital and present. Athanasius of ancient Alexandria is with the man to-day who cannot get away from the thought that whatever else Christ may be He is without doubt divine. Benedict's mood sways the conduct of men of the sixth century among the foothills of the Apennines, of men of the twentieth century on the banks of the River Charles, and of all who even temporarily leave the world to help it. Hildebrand and Pius are not only in the Rome of 1085 and 1870, but in much of the Romanism of our own land, and in the minds of the men of to-day who would see religion again as the acknowledged motive of the nations. Francis and Ignatius are the contemporaries of all those who see Christ face to face and who believe that the things of the spirit are as present and vivid as objects of sense perception.

And am I wrong in speculating as to the inner nature of this contemporaneousness? Are my debts to these and other men a mere recognition of the contributions they have made to my thought and my life? Recently, in opening an address on Cranmer, I caught myself making the unpremeditated remark—"Are these men whom I study and who are of such vital moment in my daily life a mere memory or are they a living companionship? Are they only figures of the past or are they my helpful spiritual associates?" I cannot tell. My spiritual nature is too rudimentary to venture an answer. But of this I am sure. They are much more than the content of my memory. They throng my mind as if their services were ordained and constituted in a wonderful order. The day may come when I shall dare to give a great name and a great character to my companionships with men of a former day. The inner meaning of the Transfiguration has only within the last few years begun to lay hold on me. Some day even the least of the servants of our Lord will be able to say that, like his Master, he may approach the baffling problems of life vividly conscious of the spiritual companionship of men whose experience is still at the service of those who need it.

With this personal confession I pass to a study of my six men. In each case I try to tell in what kind of an age the man lived, what kind of a man he was as he lived in it, and what, in his own way and in the language of his time, he tried to do. I trust that within these stories certain principles of permanent value may appear.

# CHAPTER II

## ATHANASIUS

THE life of Athanasius spans practically three-quarters of the fourth century. Those years, beginning in the last decade of the third century and ending in 373, include the period within which the Roman Empire passed from paganism to the public recognition of the Church. The personality of Athanasius, more than any other single agency, worked the change, not only from the old religion to the new, but from paganism to that type of Christianity which has prevailed most widely down to the present day.

Compare the situation at the close of the third century with that at the time of the death of Athanasius and one will readily see not only the change that passed over the Church, but also the conditions under which Athanasius lived and worked and in the midst of which he exercised the full strength of his religious genius.

Athanasius was born toward the end of the forty years of comparative peace which the Church had enjoyed from about the year 260, the close of the Decian-Valerian Persecution, a period within which the Church had grown with remarkable rapidity. But while Athanasius was still a boy the Diocletian-Galerian Persecution burst upon the Church with fury. Like all efforts to accomplish the impossible it was the most cruel of all the persecutions. Beginning with the year 304 it continued with intermittent intensity until 311. The State sought to attack the Church at the source of its power. Thinking that the Church could not survive without the record from which it drew its inspiration, the State ordered that the Scriptures should be surrendered. The persecutors were very thorough. Naturally some manuscripts survived and became the originals of later texts, but they were few in number and have long since ceased to be. In the systematic search that was made many of the Christians loyally refused to give up their sacred writings and were put to death for their disobedience. Others obeyed the royal command and were each given a certificate (libellus) as evidence of their subjection to the imperial will.[1] The latter were called traditors because they had betrayed the Church, and they were dropped from the rolls of the faithful. But the persecutors, not content with halfway measures, also sought out the leaders of the different Christian communities, ordered them to reverence

[1]An original libellus is in the Alexandria Museum.

the statue of the Emperor and to sacrifice to the gods. Upon their refusal to do so they were killed. The Bishop of Alexandria, whom Athanasius doubtless knew, was one of the victims. Such was the state of affairs at the opening of the century.

Glancing now at the position of the Church within the State shortly after Athanasius died, how different one finds it to be! The Emperor Theodosius himself summoned the second general council at Constantinople in 381. He gave the Church not only a secure position within the State, but he recognized its superiority to religions of other types. Thereafter Christianity and citizenship were to be almost synonymous terms. An alliance between Empire and Church had been made that was to last for centuries. Athanasianism had become official.

In its struggle with the religions of the Empire the Church was also to pass, within these years, from a position of threatened defeat to one of assured victory. Toward the close of the second and at the opening of the third centuries three men of singularly vivid and intelligent faith were, in succession, the heads of the Neoplatonic School—Ammonius Saccas, Plotinus and Porphyry. They were men whose conduct was a model of purity and unselfishness, whose religion was of profound spiritual satisfaction and whose intelligence commanded the respect of all. The headquarters of the school were in Alexandria, the native city of Athanasius. While he was young and throughout the years of his episcopate the school was flourishing, and about half a century after he died Hypatia, one of the noblest of women, was on its staff of teachers. Its appeal, however, was to those primarily of culture and mental refinement. The people at large were unaffected by it.

Mithraism, however, was of a very much more democratic character. It was a religion that had come from the east; it recognized the Sun, or Light, as its central object of worship; it emphasized the double and opposing powers of good and evil; it called for self-control and for complete personal regeneration. With surprising rapidity it spread toward the west. Espoused by the Emperors during the third century, it became the foremost religion of the State. It was received into the army; it became the faith of the soldier; it was carried by him into the parts of the Empire in which he was stationed. Its central principle being the Sun, or Light, it was international in character and therefore might easily be understood wherever the soldier might take it. Its mysteries, or secret initiations and services, its forms of worship, made a profound appeal to those who were discontented with their lives and who were seeking assurance and peace. And yet it had its limitations. It did not appeal to the intellectual classes and it left woman altogether out of account.

Such was the religious situation in Alexandria and elsewhere when Athanasius was born. Shortly after he died Neoplatonism, although still permitted by the State and still influential in Alexandria and in many other portions of the Empire, had lost its hold on many of the cultured. The Emperor Julian had sought in 361–363 to destroy the Christian Church and put a Neoplatonic Church in its place. The experiment had only to be tried to be proved impossible. Thereafter the State not only withdrew its open support from paganism, but gradually began to undermine its influence. Mithraism seemed to suffer the fate of the Roman armies. With the decreasing area of their activity it declined in its appeal. With the loss of State support, and primarily with its failure to retain the Emperor's personal embodiment of its principles, it seemed to vanish away. During the last years of the life of Athanasius men knew that a religion which made no place for woman, which was primarily a soldier's faith and which reverenced Light rather than the God who made the light could not survive.

Between the days of the youth of Athanasius and those of his old age there was also a marked difference in the internal condition of the Church. At the opening of the fourth century it was impossible to say what was the accepted point of view in regard to membership within the Church. The Novatians and the Donatists said that those only might be Church members who had never lapsed from the faith during the days of persecution. On the other hand, Rome and those who agreed with her said that both the faithful and those who had shown proper signs of contrition after their apostasy might be members.

Furthermore, during those early years of the fourth century there seemed to be almost as many ideas in regard to the person of Christ as there were thoughtful centres of Christian life and Christian speculation. Origen, a teacher in Alexandria, who had lived fifty years before Athanasius was born, had said that Christ was eternally generated of the Father. Those who laid the emphasis on the word "generated" thought that there was a time when Christ did not exist. Others, who riveted their attention on the word "eternal" were equally certain that there never was a time when Christ was not. The radical difference of opinion gave rise to many schools of thought, each one of which imagined itself thoroughly Christian. By the end of the century two general councils of the Church had defined the nature of Christ and had said that one point of view and that only might be accepted as true.

Such a definition could not have been possible

unless the Church had taken another and very important step during the lifetime of Athanasius. Previous to the year 300 no general councils had been held. Local and provincial councils only had met to deal with local and provincial questions. They had settled such matters as discipline, forms of service and expression of faith. Their conclusions, however, had weight only in their own immediate neighborhood, or in those other parts of the Church within which they commended themselves. But after Constantine gave the Church official recognition in the year 313 it was inevitable that a general council of the Church should take place. An attempt was made at Arles in 314. Representatives of the Church were summoned, but only a small proportion of them could or would come. Vital problems were considered, but, inasmuch as the representation was not complete the conclusions to which the council arrived were not thought to be universally binding. Arles, however, proved to be a kind of dress-rehearsal for the later Council of Nicæa, which met in 325. There the representation was fairly general and there problems of morals, administration and faith were discussed and brought to a solution. The universal Church had found a voice. The council's definitions were supposed to be final. And, although differences of opinion within the Church were to continue with vigor during the following two centuries and were never altogether to cease, yet there was a central authority from which one might discover, not necessarily what was the final truth, but what was the accepted point of view.

Such was the situation during the early years of the life of Athanasius and such the situation toward its end and shortly after he had died. In other words Athanasius was alive at one of the most fateful moments in the history of Christianity. With his own eyes he saw the change from the days of persecution to the days of triumph; within his own city he noticed that the State was gradually withdrawing its respect from even the finer forms of paganism and transferring it to Christianity; he himself had attended councils the purpose of which was to regulate matters of administration, morals and faith. Furthermore when he died he knew that the convictions for which he himself had always stood were likely to be generally recognized. And one does not hesitate to think that his own consistent and deeply religious nature did much to work the change.

As I have said, Athanasius was born in the last decade of the third century and Alexandria was his home. According to tradition he appeared upon the stage of history in a rather dramatic way. His bishop, Alexander, was entertaining some of the local clergy. Possibly Arius, the later opponent of both the bishop and Athanasius, was one of the number. Alexander happened to look out of his window and there on the shores below he saw some boys at play. They attracted his attention, for they were evidently "playing church." He watched them and he saw that one of them was baptizing the others. Immediately he sent one of his clergy to inquire more fully into the nature of the game and to bring to him the leader of the boys. Athanasius was brought into Alexander's house. The bishop asked him what he had been doing and in what way he had done it. The answer satisfied the bishop that Athanasius had validly baptized his playmates and he declared them members of the Church. But more than this, Alexander must have been strongly attracted to the boy. The enterprise of the young Athanasius, his evident qualities of leadership, his sincerity and enthusiasm were traits that Alexander needed within the priesthood. Tradition has it that from this time on Alexander took Athanasius into his own house, directed his education, made him his secretary and finally his chaplain, archdeacon and theologian.

It is not easy to discover how Athanasius appeared to his contemporaries and what impression he made upon them. Gregory of Nazianzus, a later contemporary of Athanasius, wrote his life. But evidently the biographer had kissed the Greek equivalent of the Blarney Stone, for the story is

GREGORY OF NAZIANZUS AND ATHANASIUS

Saec. XI

Jerusalem, Greek Patriarchal Library, Codex 14

a succession of superlatives, not all of which could possibly have been true to the facts. Nevertheless, within the heart of the story and within the reports that have come not only from other friends but from foes as well, we have the picture of a forceful man.

He was somewhat under the normal size. His hair was red. He wore moustache and beard. The beard was trimmed in Egyptian fashion—pointed and turned up at the ends, much as beards are represented in Egyptian bas-reliefs of a much earlier date. It is hard for a Westerner to picture his saint as a man of this particular type! He had eyes of depth and beauty. They had the power of piercing one's mind and soul. He carried himself well, in spite of his small stature. He was one of those small men whose masterful natures make them look large. The Emperor Julian called him the little mannikin. And it was Julian who allowed the exiled Athanasius to return to Alexandria, thinking that his presence there would again cause internal trouble in the Church and, in consequence, destroy it. Gibbon, who wasted no sympathy or respect on the early Christians, said that Athanasius was far more worthy to direct the affairs of the Empire than were any of the degenerate sons of Constantine.

Athanasius was persistent. On one occasion a council had not treated him frankly and fairly.

He appealed to the Emperor Constantine. Receiving no reply to his repeated efforts to secure the Emperor's aid he went to Constantinople, waited until the Emperor appeared in public procession, stopped the imperial horse in the middle of the street, stated his case and won Constantine's favor.

Athanasius was resourceful. His enemies had accused him of killing a bishop named Arsenius and then of cutting off the dead man's right hand and using it for purposes of sorcery. When Athanasius appeared in the council to answer the charges laid against him he brought Arsenius, heavily veiled. He asked his judges whether they would be convinced by evidence. When they said that they would, he showed them first the man, and then the man with both hands safe and sound.

Athanasius had presence of mind. While his imperial enemies were coming through one door of the Cæsareum, in which, against the imperial will, he had been holding an Easter service, he himself walked in procession out through another door. During a service in the Church of St. Theonas the soldiers entered, killed many of the congregation, and were about to murder the bishop himself when, after he had seen that his presence would no longer be of help to his people, he escaped by a rear door. On another occasion his enemies were pursuing him up the Nile. Athanasius knew that they were overtaking him, so he turned about and sailed down the river. As he slipped by the boat of his pursuers the soldiers asked him if he knew where Athanasius was. He answered that the man whom they were after was not far away.

Athanasius was also one of those men whose unique power is proved by the absurd charges brought against them. If there was a shortage in the Egyptian corn crop his enemies either honestly or dishonestly thought that he was at the bottom of it. If his clergy were seen to have a new supply of linen vestments it was said that Athanasius had laid upon the people a heavy burden of taxation. Like Wyclif and Luther, centuries after him, just because he had stirred people to think and to act, the blame for the bad as well as the good consequences of action was laid at his door. But after all, as in the case of Wyclif and Luther, there is something to be said for the charges of the enemy. Whenever men are stimulated to think, whether it be along theological lines or any other, they are likely to do some thinking along every line, and results not at all contemplated by the reformer will be brought into being, sometimes results with which the reformer would not sympathize. Athanasius was a thinker and an actor himself; the contagion of his activity made others think and act; some good and some bad thinking and acting were the consequence. It could not have been otherwise. It is to his credit, however, that he made men think.

Athanasius appeared upon the stage of history during a local religious and theological disagreement within the city of Alexandria. Bishop Alexander and one of his clergy, Arius, differed in regard to the nature of the person of Christ. If tradition be correct, Alexander had an episcopal house on the shores of what is now called the Eunostos or new harbor. It was probably situated not far from the site of the modern customs house. The only present reminders of those ancient days are the ruins of the Serapeum and Pompey's Pillar. Arius, on the other hand, lived in the court end of the town. Although the Christian Church had enjoyed only a very few years of recognition on the part of the State, there had been sufficient time to erect a Christian building in the midst of the old pagan palaces and temples. About a mile to the east of the bishop's house and church, on the shores of the old harbor, were the house and church of Arius. He was a "rector" in a fashionable locality. He was also a popular preacher. He was earnest; he was eloquent; his sermons helped. Therefore he had a large and well-earned following. It is said that the women of his congregation were those over whom he had the strongest hold. And this, although it is said to his damage, may be a point much in his favor, for, after all, the women are the mothers of men. His appearance was that of one whose sole thought was his work. He was very tall, very thin, very ascetic-looking. He was a man of spotless morality. But, like so many good men of eloquent speech, warm emotions, useful life, he was not a thinker, and, what is more to the point, his thinking whether good or bad did not commend itself to his bishop, and was destined not to appeal to the Church of the future.

Neither was Alexander a thinker primarily. He was a warm-hearted, efficient worker. But his heart and his contact with people, as well as his apprehension of the Christian tradition and the Gospel story, had led him to a conclusion in regard to the Person of Christ very different from that of Arius. It may be that at this early stage of the Alexandrian troubles Alexander was depending on the experience and the thinking of his young secretary and theologian, Athanasius.

The difference between the two lay in this: Arius said that there was a time when Christ, the Son of God, did not exist, that he was created by the Father at some time in the remote depths of eternity, and that he was not of the same nature as the Father. Neither was Christ, according to Arius, of the same nature as man. He was unlike human nature. He was, therefore, a being altogether peculiar to Himself, another god placed between God and man, between heaven and earth, less than God, greater than man. Alexander, on the other hand, held that Christ had eternally existed, that there never was a time when the Son was not, and that this Son bore the perfect human nature as well as the perfect divine nature. The points of view were, therefore, the very opposite of one another. And it was inevitable that trouble should follow.

As Alexander forbade Arius to preach such theories in regard to the Person of Christ, and as Arius refused to obey the episcopal command, the rift between the two men was complete and the townspeople took sides at once. The following of Arius was immense. His favorite ideas had become so popular that even the fishermen along the shores of the Mediterranean chanted them to familiar tunes as they went about their work. The following of Alexander, if not so large, was strong in character and in Christian experience. And more than all, it included the dauntless and spiritually-minded Athanasius. But Alexander was in a position of authority and Arius was expelled from Alexandria. Thus ended the first chapter of the controversy.

The second chapter began with the Emperor Constantine's increasing concern in regard to such a difference within the Church itself. He had made peace between the State and the Church.

Now he was not only disappointed, but somewhat angry, to hear that Christians themselves were not at peace with one another. He determined to stop the quarrel at once. His method, however, showed very clearly that he was still very much of a pagan and that he had little comprehension of the finer shades of Christian thought and feeling. A brief glance at his character will make it fairly evident that he could hardly be expected to cope with the Alexandrian troubles in an intelligent way.

Constantine's father was a Roman soldier, stationed at one time in Britain, whose religion might be called pagan monotheism. He was not far from the Christian faith, for he believed in one God. Constantine's mother, Helena, was a Christian. At the time Constantine recognized the Christian Church as one of the legal religious institutions he probably shared the religion of his father more than he did that of his mother. It is also quite probable that he was familiar with the general nature of Christianity. But neither in the days before he issued his edict of toleration nor during the period between that and his death was his Christianity anything more than a theory which he thought might be of value to the State. That he was not baptized until he lay on his death bed is no evidence that his Christianity was not vital, for many a good Christian in those days delayed baptism until the last moment, lest post-baptismal sin might condemn them to eternal punishment. The final evidence lies in the fact that Constantine was a consummate statesman. He thought of the welfare of the State before he thought of religion. The being of the State was more real to him than the being of God. And consequently that religion would appeal to him which would lend to the unity and strength of the State. He had ample opportunity to examine the religions of his day and to decide which of the many would most effectively help the State. Within the period of his own early life he had come in contact with Neoplatonism and Mithraism and the various types of Mystery Religion with which the Empire was so full. He had seen Christianity in his own home. His knowledge of the controversy between State and Church for three fateful centuries had shown him that Christianity had a secret of power shared by no other faith, and that its vitality seemed to feed on persecution. Furthermore, he saw that the despised Christians were an international brotherhood, that they were of every tribe, race and nation, and that they might be found in the remotest corners of the Empire as well as in its cities. To what conclusion could a genius of a statesman come other than that Christianity might be the fibre of the State, that an enormous empire which was already becoming unwieldy, already showing signs of internal unrest and of external hostility, might be pulled together again and become a vast civic brotherhood through the quiet and effective working of the Christian Church? Soldiers and citizens had been bound together before by the mystic power of Mithraism and by the religion which centred in the worship of the genius of the Emperor. Why should they not be bound even more closely by this dauntless religion of Jesus? Such may have been, such probably was, his way of thinking. Although his point of view boded well for the Church so far as its external tranquillity was concerned, it boded ill for its inner peace.

And yet it must not be supposed that Constantine's friendship was not of value to the Church. It is something to have an Emperor for a friend. And Constantine was every inch an emperor. He was a handsome man, standing probably over six feet in height, well-knit; his neck was too thick, but his face was strong, his glance compelling. He was fond of regal clothing and he almost never appeared in public unless he had given much time to his dress. Long, flowing silks, brightly colored, were his favorite costume. And he wore wigs and beard to match the color of his robes of state. Whenever he appeared in public he seemed something more than a man. In fact even Christians, who were cautious about their use of the word "divine," said that at such times he appeared more than human. Within the domain of his private and public duties his will was well-nigh absolute. He had inherited from the earlier Cæsars a scorn for the slow methods of political procedure that characterized a representative form of government. He knew, and rightly knew, that the Empire needed a strong hand and a quick, determined mind to guide its precarious destinies. At times he was brutal. He caused his wife, Fausta, to be executed on hardly well-grounded suspicions of her fidelity, and he had his eldest son done away with, imagining him to be plotting against the throne. These were quick, savage judgments. But let us remember that he lived long ago, that he was primarily an Emperor, that the State was of greater import to him than his family. Let us remember, too, that there have been other, and more recent, monarchs, even more ruthlessly savage within their domestic circles, who have been great kings and queens. But Constantine had certain virtues that were rare in the period within which he lived and for many centuries thereafter: he was never accused of infidelity. Such was his singular character. Doubtless he was brutal; doubtless he was careless of those of whom he ought to have been careful; he was proud; he was domineering; he may have been vain. But he ruled Rome as Henry the Eighth and Elizabeth ruled England—as if they loved it more than they loved themselves. To Constantine the Empire's welfare always came first, even when the interests of Christianity were at stake.

Being a man of such character and ambition it was inevitable that he should take a hand in the solution of the troubles at Alexandria. If they had arisen at Rome he could have been hardly more concerned, nor would he have tried more seriously to bring them to a satisfactory issue. For Alexandria was, from an imperial point of view, second in importance only to Rome. Constantinople had not yet been built. In the East Alexandria had no rival in either intellectual or religious influence. Throughout the empire its opinions were looked upon with respect. It gave the cue to the thinking of the West. And so Constantine summoned his faithful friend Hosius of Cordova, gave him a letter to Bishop Alexander and Arius and sent him away on his fateful errand. The Emperor's intentions were good. The results of his efforts as peacemaker were to show how little he had appreciated the real nature of the point at issue.

Constantine's letter may be paraphrased somewhat as follows: My dear Bishop:—I hear that there are religious troubles in Alexandria. I am sorry, for the one thing nearest my heart is the peace of the Christian Church. From the information that has come to me I should say that you and your good presbyter, Arius, were in disagreement about matters of no vital importance. In fact, you ought to be ashamed of yourselves for wasting your valuable time over a difference in the use of words. Pray get about your business, both of you. Attend to the weightier matters of the faith. So shall the Church in your great city have peace and the real purposes of the Gospel be carried out. (And may not one read between the lines: And so shall the Empire remain at peace.)

Alexander read the letter. Doubtless he showed it to Athanasius. He refused to recall Arius from exile. He knew that Constantine had stepped over into a field in which he was a stranger and within the ideas of which he was not at all at home. It is not reported what answer Hosius took back to his sovereign. But we know that the good bishop and his chaplain were determined that within the diocese of Alexandria the divine nature of Christ should be described only in words that might be used of God Himself.

These years that were now passing—from 319 to 325—were of importance in the life of Athanasius. He was still in his twenties. He had realized all the hopes that Alexander had placed in him. He had become a student and a writer. In fact it is of interest to know that the ideas that were to control him throughout his long life as Bishop of Alexandria were not only already clearly thought out, but also put in writing. Very early in life Athanasius had made himself an intelligent and an earnest defender of the Christian faith as he conceived it. The secret of such power lay in the further fact that very early in life he must have had a religious experience of profound reality, the vital effects of which were to remain with him and to direct him throughout his days. Compare, if you will, the beliefs for which he stood when he died with those he held when he was twenty-five years of age and you will see that they differed in no vital particular. How could they? While still quite young he had apparently come in contact with Christ as few others of his time had done. There was nothing for him to do but to clarify this experience to himself and to try to pass it on to others.

Constantine soon saw that Alexandria was stirred by something much more than a war of words, something much more than a war of local character. Men at opposite corners of the Empire were actively taking sides, and apparently as once they were willing to die for the faith so now they were willing to lay down their lives for either Arius or Alexander. At once Constantine's statesmanlike mind perceived that only corporate action could deal with a corporate problem. He would try again to assemble the Church, and he would spare no pains to make the gathering so widely representative that its conclusions would be universally valid. And as he had recently transferred the capital from Rome to his newly built city of Constantinople he would invite the bishops of the Church to the same neighborhood. He directed that a council should meet at Nicæa, on the Asiatic side of the Bosphorus.

No pains were to be spared to make the council a success. In those days there were excellently paved and well-policed roads throughout the Empire. The highways built for the rapid passage of the legions were quite as convenient for the goings and comings of merchants and bishops. But Constantine, never content with the least he could do, gave the bishops more than a safe-conduct along the thoroughfares. He made himself the first of that long line of benevolent churchmen who have paid the travelling expenses of those clergy who otherwise could not leave home. He had a vital matter in hand. The poor bishop was as essential to the peace of the Church as the bishop who from his private pocket or from the purse of his diocese could pay the bills.

The efforts of the Emperor coupled with the bishops' realization that vital matters were at stake brought together a notable company of men.

Neither Arius nor Athanasius could vote, for neither was a bishop. But both were present, and apparently, from the records, each was allowed to speak in council. The former was there to look after his own interests, the latter to advise Alexander. They are an interesting pair in their total unlikeness to one another, if for no other reason. The days of Arius were almost numbered; he was getting to be an old man; he was to outlive the council by only a very few years. Athanasius was scarce thirty years old; physically and mentally he was hardly in his prime; he had full forty years ahead of him. As one looks back on the council it seems as if Arius had come to give an account of the work he had done for the Church and as if Athanasius had come to make clear to all the faith that had been revealed to him and by which he purposed to live and labor.

Among the three hundred and eighteen bishops (to give the traditional number and to select only certain of the most influential and picturesque) were Hosius of Cordova, Eusebius of Cæsarea, Eusebius of Nicomedia and Spyridion of Cyprus.

As we already know, Hosius was an intimate friend of the Emperor and one in whom Constantine placed his trust. Furthermore, Hosius had been in touch with the Alexandrian troubles from the beginning. He was neither conspicuously religious nor noticeably thoughtful, but he must have had executive power, for he was at times the Emperor's representative and he was made president of the council.

Eusebius of Cæsarea was, as the title suggests, bishop of one of the oldest dioceses of the East and one of the richest in pure Christian tradition. He may not have been a man of unusual Christian spiritual experience, but he saw the good in men before he saw the evil and he was high-minded and scholarly. To him we are indebted for much of our knowledge of Christian life before the year 300, for he was the first Church historian; and to him we owe much of our knowledge of Constantine, for he was his biographer. It was to be expected that a man of such position, kind heart and ability might suggest the solution of the Alexandrian difficulties.

Eusebius of Nicomedia was, if one may reason from his later career, a man of very different type. Like many useful ecclesiastics of a later day he was conspicuous for statesmanship rather than for religion. He was one of the first of the churchmen who have been the spokesmen of the State and the personal friends and counsellors of kings. He was fond of pomp, as many a good churchman has been since his time, and as none should be ashamed to be. He apparently shared his monarch's point of view in regard to the peace of the Church as essential to the peace of the State. He could be a faithful friend, for he stood by Arius to the end. He enjoyed the intimate confidence of Constantine, for it was he who baptized the Emperor on his death-bed.

Spyridion, so far as the records go, took no prominent part in the deliberations of the council. He is, however, one who has lived in the affections of the Church quite as long as any. He is one of the honorable company of men of kind heart and fine feeling. Dean Stanley has said that the nickname "Spiro," so common in the island of Corfu, comes from the friendly Bishop of Cyprus, whose bones now lie in the soil of the former island. Dean Stanley has also given us a quaint story about him. Spyridion and his deacon had crossed from Cyprus to the mainland and were making their way on donkey-back through Asia Minor to the council. On one occasion they had slept at a roadside inn where they found other bishops who were bent on the same errand. Apparently also some of the bishops were partisans of Alexander while Spyridion and his deacon at the time, at least, favored the theories of Arius. Before dawn, doubtless after an evening spent in discussion that was probably somewhat warm, the deacon went out to catch the donkeys and get them ready for the journey. To his chagrin, even if not to his surprise, he found that the orthodox enemy had cut off the heads of his beasts. He returned at once and told the sad news to Spyridion. The good bishop, nothing daunted, went to the dead animals, prayed over them, replaced their heads and restored them to life. Then he and his happy deacon mounted and proceeded on their way. All this in the pitchy dark just before dawn! But the bishop's opportunity for wonder-working was not yet gone by, for when the first gray of dawn appeared they saw that the chestnut donkey was wearing the white head and the white donkey the chestnut head, and, on the whole, not minding the change. The donkeys were happy to be alive again, although not quite themselves, and the good men were happy each to be astride of a party-colored beast.[2]

The Emperor, in person, opened the council. Imagine the effect of such a beginning upon practically all of the bishops present! Only twenty years before Constantine's predecessors had launched against the Church the most furious and threatening of all the persecutions. And now these bishops, many of whom, doubtless, had suffered for the faith, and possibly some of whom had denied it and afterward had repented of their cowardice, were called to order by the Emperor himself. Not only this. An Emperor summoned them together who seemed to have the welfare of the Church at heart even more than many of the bishops themselves.

We have no record of what Athanasius thought of the Emperor's opening address. We may, however, make a shrewd guess as to what was passing

[2]There are various versions of this legend.

through his mind as Constantine made an eloquent plea for unity. Doubtless Athanasius was with Alexander and the other bishops when the Emperor stood before them clad in the sumptuous robes of state of which he was so fond. Doubtless he heard him deplore the dissension within the Church in matters of administration as well as in those of faith. Doubtless he heard the Emperor call for the mass of letters of complaint that had been sent to him by bishops who were at odds with other bishops. And doubtless, too, he heard the Emperor ask that a brazier might be brought, saw him thrust all the letters into it unread, watched them burn to ashes, and listened to the Emperor's request that all disagreement and hostile feeling might be consumed with the letters in which they were expressed. It was all very dramatic. Probably many, if not most, of the bishops were carried away by the imperial method. Athanasius, however, had had a religious experience. He had in some strange way come in contact with Christ. He knew Him as one knows a friend. Whether there was to be peace within the Church or not would depend altogether upon whether the bishops were going to describe the nature of Christ in the highest terms, and whether their terms would imply that whenever one listens to the words of Christ he hears the words of God, whenever one reads of the deeds of Christ he reads of the deeds of God, and whenever one looks upon the face of Christ he beholds the fulness of the Godhead bodily. Peace might be a virtue only when the consequence of a right decision, not when the result of either wrong decision or compromise. In fact he knew that the surest pathway toward peace in religion as well as in any of the higher interests of life would lie along the way of the richest experience of the profoundest natures. One can almost hear Athanasius reasoning in some such way as this. We can easily imagine him discussing with the deep-natured Alexander the Emperor's address; we can picture them reaching their decision that Constantine was still as far from a right understanding of the difficulties as he was when he wrote the letter of some years before. Athanasius and his bishop were by no means swept off their feet by the Emperor's impressive plea. They knew that there might be trouble ahead.

Nevertheless, Constantine's speech made a deep impression. With a will the bishops addressed themselves to business. They determined that there should at least be an honest effort toward a definition that should at once describe the nature of Christ and express the mind of the Church.

At the beginning of the fourth century there were many confessions of faith, or creeds, in use. For the most part they were in agreement on the essentials, but they differed in detail. Furthermore, even when such clauses as those relating to the Person of Christ varied slightly there was no necessary assumption that the variations indicated a vital difference of opinion. Many of the local creeds were expressed in such general terms that men whose views were not identical might repeat them with honesty.

Eusebius of Cæsarea saw that there was likely to be difficulty in so defining the nature of Christ that Arius and his friends and Alexander and Athanasius and their friends would be content. Possibly for many years he himself and doubtless his predecessors had used a statement of the Faith, or creed, which had satisfied spiritually a large and important section of the Church. In addition, it had come into being in a region and in a city not many miles away from Nazareth. Eusebius had every reason to think that his creed would meet the Emperor's dearest wish. He was a friend and protector of Arius. He was religiously quite as much in sympathy with Alexander. He was probably familiar with the mind of the Emperor. And so, after the rift between Arius and Alexander began to appear, he ventured to offer his creed, not as a compromise, but as a statement of rich associations to which each party might whole-heartedly agree.

It must have been to his pleasure, possibly to

his great surprise, that he found all were ready to accept it. It satisfied Arius; it satisfied Alexander. But he must have been dumbfounded to discover that the very speed with which it was welcomed raised the suspicion of Alexander and his followers. If, the latter reasoned, Arius can accept this statement there must be something wrong about it; a danger may lurk within the unguarded language; therefore, to make sure that the opinions of Arius may not be held within the Church, apparently a possibility if the creed of Eusebius were accepted, certain protecting clauses must be inserted. Consequently Alexander's party[3] asked the council to add to the creed of Eusebius the following clauses which were levelled directly against Arius: "Only begotten, that is, of the substance of the Father,"[4] and "The Holy Catholic and Apostolic Church anathematizes those who say that there was a time when the Son of God was not, and that He was not before He was begotten, and that He was made from that which did not exist; or who assert that He was of other substance or essence than the Father, or is susceptible of change." There could be no doubt about the meaning of such language. It was a challenge to the council to express itself clearly. But, strange to say, the council, almost at once, accepted the

[3]At the instance of Hosius and Constantine.
[4]And other clauses of similar import.

amendment. The Emperor, utterly unaware of the deep spiritual purpose and of the remarkable apprehension of the nature of Christ which these strange words implied, but thinking that they represented the general mind of the Church, threw in his lot with the majority. Such, then, was to be the definition. Such the Nicene Creed. Arius, naturally, being an honest man, would not subscribe to anything that so clearly condemned his thought, his teaching and himself. Constantine ordered him into exile. Eusebius of Nicomedia, after some pardonable and bewildered hesitation, honorably decided to share the fate of his friend. The council came to an end. The Church had its Confession of Faith. The Christianity of Alexander and Athanasius, the reflection of what they thought of Christ, seemed to be the mind of the Church. May not one say that nothing could stand in the way of the overwhelming conviction, the rich spiritual experience, of the young archdeacon of Alexandria? And yet there was to be no peace.

There was to be no peace because, as yet, the Church was not quite sure what it had done. In fact, for many years it seemed as if it thought that it had come to the wrong conclusion. Although it had fortunately reached a conclusion that was to commend itself to the great mass of Christians of later days the council did not meet the purpose for which Constantine had convened it. It is probably true that the council was swept off its feet by the contagious spirituality and unalterable conviction of Alexander and Athanasius rather than that it expressed the calm judgment of the majority. It did right without being fully aware of what it was about, as has been the case with so many gatherings, religious or political or social, that have reached sound conclusions. Without doubt it is true that Constantine lent the weight of his position to the Alexandrians, but it seemed for the time as if they were the spokesmen of the majority, at any rate of the plurality, for the anti-Alexandrians were of many shades of opinion while the Alexandrians were a unit in their belief. However, very few months had passed by before not only Constantine, but Christians throughout the Empire, perceived that the council's decision was not representative. The tragedy of it was that the bulk of the East, at any rate, could not grasp the spiritual meaning of the words for which Athanasius had fought.

As we of to-day look back on that decision we see that it expressed the richest of the many ideas in regard to the Person of Christ, and that, in consequence, the decision would hold. But to Constantine and his contemporaries the result did not so appear. All that they could see was a Church the leaders of which quickly returned to their previous points of view. It even seemed to them that, after all, Arius might be right, and that unity might be discovered along the pathway of agreement with him. As most of them were still semi-pagans not only was this quite natural, but it should have been expected. The pre-Conciliar confusion was now worse confounded. The thin, meagre spiritual experience of the majority of the bishops and of the State could not fathom the mature and rich faith of Athanasius. Shortly after the council, Athanasius, almost literally, stood alone, *contra mundum.* Fifty years were to pass before the Church was to realize that it had builded better than it knew, before it developed into an appreciation of its action. Half a century of religious and theological and imperial unrest was to be endured before the Church, with anything like unanimity, could accept the faith as Athanasius conceived it.

From the end of the council of Nicæa until the death of Athanasius—from 325 to 373—the mood of the Church and of the State in its relation to the Church may be seen in the experiences through which Athanasius passed.

Alexander died shortly after the return to Alexandria. With the enthusiastic and general approval of clergy and laity Athanasius succeeded him. He was hardly thirty years old. But he was mature beyond his years, like the profound in heart who are always mature, young though they may be. Now, after ten years of devoted service, he was not only to think out the policies of the diocese of Alexandria and not only was he to lead men to their fulfilment, but he was also to be the imperial symbol of the misunderstood right conception of the Person of Christ. He was ready for the future, whatever it might have in store.

As the momentum of the decision at Nicæa did not immediately die away Athanasius was allowed to go about his episcopal work unmolested. At length Constantine, bewildered by the unexpected turn of events and still eager for peace, asked the young bishop to restore Arius to his diocese and Church. Athanasius at once and finally refused to reinstate a man whose views had not changed in the slightest, and who, in his judgment, was distinctly unchristian. The Emperor retaliated by banishing Athanasius. The sentence proved at once that Constantine had turned Arian and that Athanasius was to have no freedom throughout the rest of the Emperor's reign. But, as always, Athanasius made capital of his misfortunes. Tréves, the place of his exile, was in the heart of the Roman colonial West; temperamentally the West had always leaned strongly toward the idea of Christ for which Athanasius stood; many of the leaders of the Western Church warmly espoused his cause as their own; he himself, knowing that his faith was of far more than diocesan significance, never failed to summon men to its acceptance. But the situation in which he was, an exile, the general sympathy of the West for his cause, the bitter hostility of much of the East and of the Emperor, were more than personal—they were indications of the mood of Church and State.

When Constantine died in 337 it seemed for a moment that Athanasius was to be allowed not only to return, but to live and work in peace. As the sons of Constantine were divided in their religious allegiance it might be that Athanasius would profit by the lack of a united policy. Such, however, was not to be the case. The Arian Constantius was to rule the East. He was no sooner firmly seated on his throne with Eusebius of Nicomedia as Bishop of Constantinople than Athanasius was driven forth again. Knowing the mood of the West he again made that the place of exile. He appealed to men of influence. His cause was brought before councils. He was aware that the bulk of the West was in sympathy with him. But he also learned that the larger portion of the East was possibly farther away from him than ever and that they could not countenance the conclusions of any councils of the West. Nevertheless, after six years of exile and at a moment when Arianism itself was losing in popularity and, therefore, was gradually proving itself not to be the religion of the Empire, and when Constantius seems to have become weary of his fruitless opposition, Athanasius was allowed to go home.

There was little doubt as to how his fellow-citizens felt about him. With pardonable candor he himself tells us how they received him on one of his returns from exile. "The people ran in crowds to see his face; the Churches were full of rejoicing; thanksgivings were offered up everywhere; the ministers and clergy thought the day the happiest in their lives." On another return the crowd that came out to welcome him resembled "another Nile." Without question he was the hero of the Alexandrians. And with reason. He gave himself freely to them. They knew that he was unselfish and high-minded. They knew that with Athanasius to live was Christ.

The second return of Athanasius, however, revealed an interesting mood of Constantius, the Empire and the Church. It seemed to be one of irritation rather than of clear-cut intelligent policy. Athanasius must be disposed of, got rid of. Possibly force would do the work. Hence the soldiers were sent to take him. It was on this occasion that he slipped out of the church by a rear door and fled away up the Nile. Again his adversity was turned to good account, for he went to his good friends the monks of the desert. And there among the barren hills, lovely in their color and their quiet, grand in their desolation, he lived the life he loved so well—one of self-restraint, of study, of contemplation and prayer. One needs only to walk among those hills to cease to pity the exile and envy him his companionship with God. During this period he wrote his Orations against the Arians, a carefully prepared statement of his point of view, and there, not far from the region in which Anthony, the first Christian monk, had lived and had exerted his wide influence, he probably gathered the material for his life of the saint.[5]

When Julian the Apostate came to the throne in 361 Athanasius was again allowed to go back to his people. Julian allowed him to do so, not for any love of Athanasius, but rather because he despised the Christian Church and was looking for some speedy and thorough way to destroy it. He had thought that the return of Athanasius would again stir up party strife, that Christians would again be at each others' throats, that fraternal hatreds would achieve their inevitable results. Although the very earnest, high-minded and scholarly Emperor reigned for only two short years the period was long enough to teach him that the Christian Church had a principle within it that could not be destroyed and that Athanasius was very precious to the Alexandrians. In

[5]If it is true that Athanasius is the author.

desperation he again drove him forth. It was one of the Emperor's last and most futile attempts to destroy Christianity and to restore paganism of the Neoplatonic type. As Julian lay dying on an eastern battle-field he is reported to have said, "Thou hast conquered, O Galilean!" It is not altogether unreasonable to suppose that the thought of Athanasius passed through his mind as he acknowledged that he was vanquished, for none of the Emperor's Christian contemporaries could match the Bishop of Alexandria in the victorious quality of his faith.

Athanasius withdrew into this his next to last exile telling his loyal and discouraged people that what seemed like a storm was only a cloud passing across the face of the sun. He was soon back at his work again. Once more he tasted the bitterness of banishment, but for a very short time, when the Emperor Valens, imagining, like Constantine and Constantius, that Arianism was to be the State religion, used him as a victim. But with the coming of Jovian the skies had cleared, the imperial opposition had passed, never to return, and Athanasius went home to Alexandria, there to live and work in comparative peace for the last ten years of his life.

As I have tried to say, it is extraordinary with what clearness one can read the signs of the times in the experience of the Alexandrian bishop. While

Constantine imagined the decision of Nicæa to be the mind of the Church Athanasius was undisturbed. But when he thought that it had reached the wrong conclusion and that Arius was right Athanasius was banished. While Constantius was determining his own policy Athanasius went about his diocese doing good. But as soon as the moment arrived when the new monarch believed the young bishop's views to be the fountain-head of disunity away Athanasius was driven again. During the years when the imperial policy showed signs of becoming gross, when those marks of irritation appeared which invariably preceded the acknowledgment of defeat, soldiers searched a church and a desert for Athanasius. When an emperor was looking for the one man, who by his unyielding faith could destroy the Church, by his uncompromising belief could divide the Church into fratricidal parties, he permitted Athanasius to exercise his full freedom. When another emperor, with the advantage of a longer perspective, reviewed the struggle and wanted to encourage the hero he gave Athanasius the comfort of a kindly word. Lastly, when Theodosius, eight years after the death of Athanasius, summoned the second general council and approved of its conclusions, he and the bishops defined the Faith in the terms that expressed the spiritual experience of Athanasius. In the varying phases of imperial policy one may readily discover the moods of the Church. State and Church took well-nigh fifty years in living into and up to the idea of Christ to which Athanasius with mind and soul had responded when hardly more than a boy, to which, without shadow of turning, he had been loyal at Nicæa, throughout the daily routine at Alexandria and the well-used years of five exiles, and down to the day of his death.

The Church was at length awake to the meaning of its own decision at Nicæa. It had developed into the mind, or rather, it had become conscious of the spiritual experience, of Athanasius as its own. And when the Christian of to-day repeats the Nicene Creed and uses the phrase "of one substance with the Father" he is not merely employing Greek terms to express a theological idea, he is rather trying, in language scarcely adequate to the purpose, to declare that Athanasius was right—that the divine nature of our Lord can be described only in terms that might be used of God. Like Athanasius he asserts that whenever he listens to the words of Christ he hears the words of God, whenever he reads of the deeds of Christ he reads of the works of God, whenever he sees the face of Christ he beholds the fulness of the Godhead bodily.

## CHAPTER III

### BENEDICT OF NURSIA

In a very real sense Benedict was a successor of Athanasius. Like practically all the men of the West he had accepted without question the warm and rich religion of Athanasius. But beyond this, he had probably found in Athanasius an earlier lover and student of the monastic way of living. It will be remembered that Athanasius spent a number of the years of his exile among the monks of the Upper Nile, that there he threw himself with enthusiasm into the life of study, of contemplation and of prayer, and that there he may have gathered material for a life of Anthony, the first Christian hermit-monk. It is most probable that Benedict was thoroughly familiar with the daily life of Athanasius and with his devotion to the monastic ideal, for not only was Benedict a student of the kinds of monasticism that had filled the brief two hundred years of its history before his day, but he himself was born only about one hundred years after Athanasius died. Athanasius and Benedict were almost contemporaries.

Furthermore, when one penetrates the heart of

a great man one wonders what he might have been if he had not been what he was. It is not always calm purpose that determines the course of a man's life. Frequently circumstances force into an unexpected channel the abilities which men of power possess. Athanasius was Alexander's secretary and chaplain and theologian; he became the voice of vast numbers of Christians; he was an imperial leader. But it is interesting to speculate as to what he might have preferred to be had he had his own way. A student, a thinker, a man of imagination, of unselfishness and self-restraint, and of passionate devotion to duty and to ideals, and a man of vast patience, he might have made to Christian living other contributions than those for which we are indebted to him. He might well have been the organizer of Christian monasticism in a rich and enduring form. Far up the Nile, in the desert haunts he loved so well, among men of kindred experience and of kindred interests he might have made a centre for contemplation and prayer; he might have gathered about him those who would work with their hands for their own support, who would be glad to call nothing their own and who, as time went on, would, in the case of certain of the more intelligent, devote themselves to study. But Athanasius resisted all these perfectly possible temptations and gave himself freely to another kind of life.

Indirectly, at any rate, Athanasius was a forerunner of Benedict, for monasticism was one of the next of the inevitable steps which Christians would take to complete their equipment for the further conversion of East and West. To have the Faith defined in a way satisfactory to the bulk of Christians throughout the world was a significant step to have taken. It now remained to develop an institution which would, as years passed by, preserve, clarify and enrich the Faith, and to raise up generations of men whose lives would embody the Christian ideal. Within the monasteries, for generations to come, the faith of Athanasius was to find its ablest representatives in life and thought.

Benedict of Nursia was the founder of the Order of Benedictine Monks. He reduced to a system the many rules that obtained during and before his own day, adding to them other regulations of common sense and wisdom. One of the historians has said of him that his monastery at Monte Cassino was as much the goal of faithful Christian pilgrims as was Rome or Jerusalem. Dante has placed him in the circle of the Rose together with the supreme Doctor of the Church, Augustine, and the saint who so closely resembled Christ, Francis of Assisi.[1] He was a man of simple, straightforward and affectionate nature, of

[1]*Paradise,* XXXII.

conspicuous executive ability, of spiritual insight, one who seemed to live in two worlds, the earthly and the heavenly.

Benedict was born in about the year 480. He died shortly before the year 550.[2] He lived, therefore, in a turbulent and dramatic period of what one may loosely call Italian history—the period in which Theodoric the Ostrogoth and his immediate successors held their precarious sway in the Italian peninsula. It was a time of almost constant war, and one in which an earnest youth might be pardonably tempted to quit society, and when an unselfish man might think he could best serve the world by leaving it.

The monastic life makes a strong appeal even to those least monastically inclined. Little as we may care to confess it, each one of us has a slight leaning toward it, and frequently we have a profound respect for the men and women of past and present who have followed or are following that way. It has an element of self-control that demands our reverence. At times it manifests a heroism that calls for our admiration. We know that perfect self-mastery is a sign of manliness. We know that even those men who have seemed guilty of exaggerating this virtue have conquered themselves. They may have swung too far, but at least they have helped to secure a proper average when

[2] 543 is the date usually given.

society seems to have swung too far in the other direction. And then, too, we confess that the life of contemplation is one that we would have the courage to lead, to a certain extent, every day. To take the opportunity to get away by ourselves, to sit or kneel in tranquillity, to accommodate our minds to the thought of God, to try to fix before our spiritual vision the character of God—these we know are eternally right, for they bring a satisfaction to the soul that we can never get by being forever about our business. We respect such a life within ourselves; we admire it in those who have been and are masters of this spiritual art; we recognize that even in its extreme forms it has an element of profound significance; we see it impressively illustrated, if not among monks in general, most surely among the creators of the monastic ideal.

For nearly three hundred years after Christ no monk appeared within the Christian church. It was not necessary that he should. The daily life of the average Christian called for the kind of character and conduct that seemed to gratify the Christian longing for the unusual. The personal influence of Christ was still strong; of necessity the Christian lived apart from the world; he was in almost daily danger of being slaughtered for his faith. His thought and conduct were unlike those of his pagan acquaintances and fellow-citizens.

But as time wore on, and particularly during the lengthening periods between the persecutions and the constantly retreating influence of the Person of Christ on the average man, the standard of thought and conduct seemed somewhat to decline. At this moment the clergy began to represent the higher type of life. As the people in general identified themselves more closely with the normal routine of citizenship, the clergy were the ones to follow the separated and peculiarly Christian kind of life. But toward the end of the long peace, 260–300, and after Constantine put Christianity on a plane of equality with other religions, the clergy themselves became most respectable members of society, so respectable in fact that they were given such privileges as a partial support at the expense of the State and freedom from many of the duties exacted of the laity. In other words, the entire Church felt at home in the State, and only with difficulty could the respectable Christian be distinguished from the respectable pagan. As always under similar conditions, a movement began within the Church the purpose of which was to preserve the Christian from too close a conformity to the ordinary standards of the day. And also, as always, the conformity being very complete, the reaction was very extreme—toward the end of the third century Anthony, the first Christian hermit, appeared.

Early Christian monasticism may be divided roughly into three classes—the hermit, the informal community and the loosely regulated community. They followed each other in rapid succession, the first two continuing while the process of more careful organization was going on. No sooner had Anthony gone into the Egyptian desert, seeking to be altogether away from the world and alone with God, than Christians went out in throngs to see him and to listen to his counsel. They found in him the example of extraordinary self-mastery and vivid consciousness of God. And although the vast majority neither expected to follow his lead nor would do so if they could, in some instinctive way they knew that Anthony, by virtue of his abnormal conduct, was elevating the tone of the Church; they leaned upon his experience; they were themselves a little less normal because he was so abnormal. The influence of the man, however, did not stop with this generally pervasive effect. Many individuals wanted to follow his example. And throughout the desert, not far from Anthony, other hermits built their huts and lived the life of isolation.

It was a natural and an easy step from the first to the second stage of monasticism. Pachomius, a later contemporary of Anthony, living on the Upper Nile not far from the town now called Esneh, saw that hermits now and then liked to get together for prayer and praise and mutual encouragement, and that certain of these hermits preferred to be always near their fellows. Apparently with imagination and wisdom he met the need. Before he died in 345 there were nine monasteries under his direction with several hundreds of monks, living together in groups of thirty or forty in separate houses, each house having its own head, the inmates eating, sleeping, praying and praising together. They were extreme or not in their austerities as they pleased. They plied practically all of the well-known trades. In fact, apart from much of the voluntariness of the system, the Pachomian monasticism resembled very closely that of a much later day.

In Asia Minor, however, and Syria, the hermit-type was the more popular, and wherever there were, in the later fourth century, well established communities degeneration seems to have set in. Basil of Cæsarea, the organizer of Eastern monasticism, seems to have realized that degeneration was due to lack of a purpose in the monastic life. He therefore brought his monks near the cities, regulated their day and made them care for the sick. What Basil did for the East, Cassianus of Marseilles did for the West. The latter had been a great student of the different kinds of monasticism; he knew that the West lacked form and purpose. He therefore drew up rules and organized the monastic life on what might be called a system of advice or recommendations of the way men were to live either in a community or as hermits.

Cassianus died about forty-five years before Benedict was born, and as he had himself leaned strongly toward the extreme Egyptian form of monastic life, a reformer was yet to come who would do for the West the kind of pioneering work that would make the monk useful to society in a very practical sense of the word.

The world within which Benedict lived created a heavy demand for an extraordinary type of Christian life. He was born and he died within the very heart of the period of the Barbarian invasions—or migrations, as they are more correctly termed. Between the years 400 and 600, to speak in round numbers, the successive waves of migration had flooded over the Western Empire. The Vandals had swept around through Spain into Northern Africa; the Visigoths had entered, conquered and settled in Spain; the Ostrogoths had remained in the Balkan Peninsula and in Italy; the Lombards in Northern Italy. The Angles, Saxons and Jutes had become masters of southern England. Yielding to the terrific pressure, the Roman provincial armies had withdrawn from England early in the fifth century and from most of France at the beginning of the sixth. A movement was taking place destined completely to change the character of the West. The old Roman provincial peoples were suppressed, the old Roman culture passed away, and in their place appeared a barbarian civilization, crude, but young, vigorous and enthusiastic. A stratum of fresh, ignorant and spontaneous enterprise was spread upon the old stratum of decadent and over-refined Roman provincialism. All this was taking place just before Benedict was born, while he lived, and just after he died. His own biographer, Pope Gregory I, was the first to analyze the changing conditions and in a masterly way to accept them and to try to give them a right direction. What more natural, then, than that one living in those turbulent times not only should think that he could not find God among men and therefore should abandon the city for the country, but also that he should in the country create a centre where even the most warlike of the barbarians should become aware of the presence of God.

I have just mentioned the name of Gregory the Great, Pope of Rome from 590 to 604, and I have said that he was Benedict's biographer. We know very little about Benedict beyond what Gregory has told us. It is a story written with reverence and affection by a truly great man of his truly great spiritual father. Gregory was, according to the standards of his day, a scholar; he had remarkable executive ability; he was a far-seeing and highly intelligent statesman. But at heart he was a monk. He might have had high rank in the State if he had remained a layman, or if he had been willing to remain in the offices of State and Church in which he had won an enviable reputation. But he followed the dictates of his heart when he turned his father's house on the Caelian Hill into a monastery, when he set out for England to turn to Christianity the Anglo-Saxon barbarians, and when, being summoned back after he was well on his way, he sent a monk of his own monastery in his stead.

It is from such an affectionate monastic heart that our knowledge of Benedict comes. It is a story filled with miracle. As Mr. Hodgkin has said, the wonders told in it are in certain cases beyond the belief of the most credulous Romanist. But it is a story that reveals the deepest respect, veneration and affection of the one who wrote it, and within the most improbable parts of which one may find evidence of a man whose powers were far beyond those of his fellows. Miracles of kindness and love are not reported of either small or average natures.

It is not uninteresting to remember that through Gregory, English and American Christians come into close touch with Benedict. For, as I have said, it was Gregory who wanted to go to England. It was he who sent the Benedictine monk Augustine. It was a group of Benedictine monks who landed on the southeastern coast of England and who marched across the fields and through the woods of Kent, chanting their litanies, until they reached their future home at Canterbury.

Benedict was born in the small but picturesquely situated town of Nursia[3] about seventy-five miles northeast of Rome. It nestles under the shadow of the Sibillini mountains, the highest of the Apennines, and it forms the northern apex of the approximately seventy-five mile triangle—Nursia, Rome, Monte Cassino, within which his remarkable life was lived and outside of which the good man never stepped. It might be added that it was a region of singular beauty, for Nursia, Rome and Monte Cassino are lovely and grand portions of a land that everywhere appeals to the heart and the imagination.

Benedict was of gentle blood, for his parents were of noble lineage. Undoubtedly he enjoyed as a child the advantages of education and of culture common to his class, meagre though they may have been in that day of crumbling civilization. Even in his boyhood he seemed mature; he had no taste for the usual occupations of youth. Like John Stuart Mill and John Henry Newman

[3]The modern Norcia.

he had neither time nor inclination to play.[4] When he was about fifteen years old his parents sent him to Rome where, under more advantageous circumstances, he might continue his education. Doubtless they were following the method common to the country nobility of the day in the education of their boys. Apparently also his parents and his twin sister Scholastica went to Rome with him, for there is a strong Roman tradition that the family city home was in the present Piazza Piscinæla, across the Tiber from the Palatine Hill.

The boy himself, however, was doing some thinking about his future. He took the measure of his new companions and of the subjects he was studying and of the city in which he was passing his time. He thoroughly distrusted and disliked his new way of living. He seemed afraid that he himself would yield to the temptation to become careless and possibly dissolute. And, may not one add that possibly he missed the mountains, the sky and the open reaches of the country to which he had been accustomed from his birth and to which he returned at both Subiaco and Monte Cassino? At all events he left home and school and wandered away into the country, across the Campagna, beyond the hills of Tivoli and into the foot-hills of the Abruzzi, about twenty-five miles

[4]Ab ipso suae puriliae tempore cor gerens senile. Aetatem quippe moribus transiens, nulli animum voluptati dedit. Ex libro II, *Dialogorum S. Gegorli magni* excerpta.

farther up the valley of the Aniene. It is a rugged, a grand and a lovely region—a broad and fertile valley, mountains rising on all sides, deep gorges between them, and the clear and rapidly running river Aniene taking their waters to the sea. Benedict saw it all and loved it. At last he was at home again, if not in the beauty of it all, at least in its comforting isolation. "Wisely ignorant and ignorantly wise," as Gregory has described him at this period, Benedict began the life that he was to follow to the end.

A good friend went with him for part of the way. It was his nurse. The singular companionship may be proof of Benedict's extreme youth. It may be evidence that Benedict's family looked upon his conduct as a passing whim of early manhood. It may have been a sign that the nurse loved him and that she wanted to follow and protect him, intending always to be within reach, always ready to help. She, like many a good nurse, may have been the only one who understood him. At any rate, it was because of her that the people of the valley began to realize who had come among them. The hospitable peasants had given them food and shelter. Accidentally the nurse had brushed against an earthenware sieve. It fell to the floor and broke. Seeing her grief, Benedict gathered up the pieces, prayed, and, according to Gregory, made the sieve as good as new, without even a mark to show that it had been broken. The incident at once gave him a reputation for sanctity throughout the countryside.

But Benedict did not want reputation among men. He wanted isolation with God. Escaping from the people and also from his good nurse, he pressed on farther up into the valley until he came to the spot where the Aniene issues from a gorge between the steep-sided mountains, and where Nero, the brutal but beauty-loving Emperor, had had a villa and had made an artificial lake. As he wandered about in search of a region in which he might be far away from men, he met a monk named Romanus, who had come down into the valley from his monastery on the brow of the mountain. At once Romanus was drawn toward the youth. At once he recognized his holiness and his pure purpose. At once he determined to do what he could to help him. Romanus led Benedict farther into the gorgelike valley above the ruined villa and the lake, climbed well up the slopes and crags and then showed Benedict a cave in the most precipitous part of the mountain-side. At last Benedict had found the retreat for which he had longed. At last he and God might be alone together. Not even his faithful nurse would know where he was. Clothed in the monastic habit which Romanus had given him he was at peace.

Romanus was a true friend. He left Benedict

to himself, but he saw to it that the boy had food from time to time. As Romanus sat at the monastic table, he would slip some food into his pocket (thereby running the risk of severe discipline). He would then take it to the top of the cliff, only a short walk from the monastery, put it into a basket to which a bell was fixed, and then lower it to the opening of Benedict's cave. Hearing the bell tinkle Benedict would come for his food. How long the kind offices of Romanus continued we do not know. The time came, however, when the basket was no longer lowered and Benedict did not know how to find even enough to keep body and soul together.

At about this time some peasants happened to stroll close to the cave. They saw in a thicket nearby what they thought was a wild animal. Coming nearer they found it was a man. They gave him food and then they listened while Benedict talked of God. As Gregory quaintly puts it, "When they had given him food for the body they received from him nourishment for the soul."[5]

Benedict, however, was not as yet altogether master of himself. His manhood was beginning to assert itself. Terrific temptations shook him to his very soul. He was on the point of yielding, of going back to Rome and of doing as the young men of his day were doing. But at a moment

[5]*Dial.*, II. *Greg.*, cap. II.

*Photo, Alinari.*

BENEDICT'S MONASTIC MEAL

From the fresco by Sodoma in the cloister of Monte Oliveto Maggiore, Siena

when the temptations were peculiarly severe, he tore his garments from his body, threw himself into a thicket of thorns and rolled about in it until his flesh was a mass of wounds. Never afterward did such temptations return. The thicket is now a garden of roses.

As Benedict's reputation spread down the valley some monks whose abbot had died thought that they would like such a saint for their leader. They came to Benedict and persuaded him, much against his will, to yield to their wish. The men were rough in mind and soul. Benedict knew that they could not lead the life he would demand of them. And so it turned out. Very quickly they began to chafe under his strict discipline and they sought to do away with him. They gave him a poisonous drink in a glass vase. As was his custom before eating or drinking, Benedict made the sign of the cross before he allowed his lips to touch the cup. Immediately the cup broke in pieces and fell to the ground. Perceiving their wickedness, Benedict abandoned them and went back to his cave.

But even then fate was against his living a life of spiritual seclusion. His fame had passed farther down the valley and into Rome itself. Pilgrimages were made to Subiaco and to the Sacro Speco—the cave in the cliff. Not only Romans but Goths came out to see and to hear him. Noblemen brought their sons and urged Benedict to take them under his care. As his reputation for wisdom and holiness grew, many youths and men came out and gave themselves to the monastic life. Seeing their need of him Benedict yielded to the evident directing hand of Providence. He left his cave, and went up higher among the mountains, and there as the years passed by he founded twelve houses, each with its own head, while he himself, their general director, lived with a few chosen friends in the thirteenth. Among those who were in closest sympathy with him were Maurus and Placidus, whose fathers had asked Benedict to receive them into the monastic life. They were to become his staunchest friends and those in whom he placed implicit confidence.[6]

The work grew, the monasteries flourished, the hermit became the centre of community life. In an age when all was despair and war, Benedict and his monasteries were the centre of hope and peace. It would seem as if such simple, straightforward goodness would have stirred among those who came in contact with it only a feeling of kindliness. Such, however, was not the case. The jealousy of a neighboring abbot, Florentius, threatened unrest and disorder, if not the ruin of Benedict's ideal of life. The evil-minded man, who

[6]Sodoma and Signorelli have made this friendship the subject of many paintings.

hated success unless he himself were the author of it, strove in every way to kill Benedict and to lay before his monks temptations too strong to resist. He sent Benedict some poisoned bread which the latter, suspecting the foul purpose, gave to a pet crow, telling him to take it to a place where no man could find it.[7] Gregory says that when Benedict realized that Florentius was burning with hatred, he was more sorry for Florentius than he was for himself.[8] Seeing that his plot against Benedict had failed, Florentius sent disreputable women to the monasteries, hoping that in this way he might show the world how weak the leadership of Benedict was.

Florentius did not succeed in destroying the work of Benedict. But he hastened Benedict's departure from Subiaco and therefore the building of the monastery at Monte Cassino. As one reads the story as told by Gregory, one would think that this was the sole cause of his leaving the neighborhood. But it was not like Benedict to turn his back upon difficulty nor to abandon friends when they were having a hard time. The trouble caused by Florentius may have been the occasion of his leaving, but underlying the occasion there was probably a deeper cause. He was at heart still much of a hermit; he was convinced that his way

[7]To this day pet crows are kept at Subiaco and Monte Cassino.
[8]*Dial.* II, p. 178.

of spending his life was not in quarrels with neighbors but in quiet companionship with those of kindred spirit and with God. Before Benedict had gone far on his way to his new monastic home, Maurus overtook him and exultantly told him to return because Florentius had been killed by an earthquake. Not only did Benedict refuse, but he punished Maurus for rejoicing at the death of an enemy. No, the good man wanted to be farther away from every one and nearer to his heavenly Father. Never again was he to be disturbed in the same way, but he was to discover that his new isolation was to be well known among men. Even the barbarian invader was to come to see him.

When Benedict and his chosen companions left Subiaco they took their way through the mountains toward the southeast and after a walk of about fifty miles they came to a high and steep hill which arose abruptly back of the Roman town of Casinum. Monte Cassino, as it has been called for many centuries, is the third and the last of the beautiful parts of Italy in which Benedict lived. It could hardly be more beautiful. It stands as a great headland jutting out into the valley of the Garigliano. At its base a flat and fertile valley spreads away on three sides to a distance of many miles. Behind it rises Mt. Cairo to an altitude of five thousand four hundred and eighty feet and far away toward the southwest, when the weather is exceptionally clear, one may catch a glimpse of the sea. In those days the Via Latina, or Latin Way, ran by its base from Rome to the south. At present the railway follows practically the same route.[9] It is lovely and grand. It is also isolated. Did it appeal to Benedict solely because of its isolation? Or is the choice of this spot another instance of monastic love of beauty and grandeur?

The monks set to work at once not only to build their new home, but to turn to Christianity the remnant of paganism which had survived at Monte Cassino long after it had disappeared from most of the Roman world. They cut down the sacred grove and pulled down the temple of Apollo that crowned the hill, and on the ruins of the temple they built their chapel. What had been a stronghold of an ancient and dying faith, surviving so long because of its isolation, was now to become the most vital centre in the West for the young and contagious religion of Jesus, destined to become very powerful because so far removed from the conflicting currents of the contemporary barbarous society.

The secret of the influence of any society never lies so much in its rules or constitution as in the personality of its founder. The rules and the constitution are at best only an attempt to organize

[9]One may see the monastery from the railway, on the left about half way between Rome and Naples.

and perpetuate the secret of a man's, or of men's, grasp of spiritual things, be they political or religious—Benedict was Benedictinism. In the early days it was great because he was great. And yet the rule itself was, for the time in which it was written, of singular value to society; and for those whose spirituality finds satisfaction in it to-day, it is of profound significance. It would seem as if Benedict had been able to infuse into his rule a generous measure of his common sense, his wisdom and affection. He apparently was master of the many types of the monastic life which prevailed in and before his time. He allowed them to filter through his own heart and mind and soul until they were made pure and wise and unselfish. When he went to Monte Cassino in about 527, he carried with him a wealth of experience in monastic life. He had been a hermit for at least three years; he had been the abbot of rough and unruly men; he had for many years controlled twelve monasteries and he had, although "wisely ignorant and ignorantly wise," been the custodian of boys and the adviser of the nobility in regard to the education of their sons. If experience plus an utterly unselfish character and a pure purpose may qualify one for leadership, surely few men were more ready than he to help society.

Four fundamental vows underlay the Benedictine rule. Three of them were common to many of the rules that were drawn up before Benedict's time—poverty, celibacy, and obedience. One was peculiar to Benedict himself—stability. The monks were to have no property of their own either in cash or in kind. Everything they had and used and wore was the monastery's. They were to be free from any of the subtle distractions that come not only from ownership but from the acquisition and holding of property. They were to be unmarried. They were not to have a double allegiance, one to their work and another to their families. They were not to be subject to the peculiar temptation to acquire property and position for the sake of wives and children. They were to obey. On their admission into full membership they were to will to abandon their wills to the head of the monastery. They were not to delay action by either wondering whether the abbot was right or by hesitating to carry out his commands. These were the three well-known primary vows. They also promised that they would never leave the monastery without the permission of the abbot. They took the vow of stability. They would not yield to the spirit of restlessness, nor would they make nuisances of themselves, as so many monks had done and were still doing, by begging from door to door and by interfering with the work of the parish clergy. They would remain in one spot and there live a thorough life. This would be the best preparation for duties away from the monastery, if the abbot gave them any such commissions, and this he did from time to time with conspicuous success.

Such rules seem rather formidable to the average man. We must remember, however, that generally only those men took the vows who were temperamentally drawn to that kind of life, and that in many ways the rewards of community life as conceived by Benedict were more satisfying than the returns from occupations in civil society. One might say that this is true of monasticism of both past and present. But it was peculiarly true in Benedict's day when civil society seemed to have lost whatever of idealism it had had. Furthermore, if one will closely examine the whole Benedictine rule he will find it a very human kind of document, and however little he may care to follow it himself, he will understand how well adapted it was for the purpose it was intended to fulfil. Benedict, as I have said, was a man of wide and deep experience. He prefaced his rule by saying he hoped he was recommending nothing too hard for the normal man to undertake.

Taking the rule as a whole one will notice two characteristics—the welfare of the individual monk should always be kept in mind; the monk should be temperate in all things. Such qualities were a novelty in Benedict's day. However, they prevailed not only on paper but in action. As to the first—if the climate was cold or warm the monk was to dress accordingly; if the days were clear and cool or sultry and hot, the hours of rest and work were to be adapted to such changing conditions. If a monk was ill he should have rest and a proper diet. Our ideas as to diet may differ from Benedict's, for meat was reserved for the sick, but we respect his point of view, and his solicitous care for those who were at all out of sorts. The second quality of the rule flows very naturally from the first. In order that the monk might always be ready for the duties of the day, that his body might be the perfect servant of his mind and spirit and that religion might be the heart of life, there must be a delicate adjustment of sleep, food, work and prayer. No one item should be exaggerated at the expense of any other. All were essential to the man. An over-indulgence in the exercises of religion would throw him out of balance as effectively as an unwise economy in sleep or food.

Looking now at the rule in detail one will see how these qualities direct and govern the routine of monastic conduct. Taken together they form an element of supreme common sense which pervades the entire document.

The rule enjoined the monks to pray. It was not enough to tell them to pray; they were told how to pray. Prayer was not the mere repetition of words, sacred though they might be. Neither was it a temporary earnest effort to commune with God. Prayer was rather the thoughtful language of the pure in heart consciously directed to God.

The monks were to praise God—to sing. Their singing would be mere noise unless they brought body, mind and soul into action in their praising. They were to sing standing, and standing erect, with their minds set on the words. The whole man was to sing and not only the voice.

The monks were to work—work with their heads and hands. It was not until somewhat later that Benedictine study, following the lead of Cassiodorus,[10] was of a scholarly character. In the earliest days it consisted largely of mastering the contents of the Bible and of early Christian writings. This they were to do thoroughly—using their minds while they did it. They were also to labor in the fields and garden. In this requirement there was evidently a double purpose. It was necessary to keep the monastic table well supplied and to maintain the monastic estate in good order. But, in addition to this, Benedict undoubtedly knew that contact with the soil and manual labor of any useful kind have a wholesome influence on mind and soul. Anyone who has

[10]Secretary to Theodoric, a scholar who toward the end of his life became a monk.

cared for his own garden and swept his own sidewalk will perceive not only the utility but the wisdom of Benedict's inclusion of work with the hands within the daily programme. The better circulation of the blood, the contentment that comes of seeing the results of one's work, keep one sane and normal at whatever task he may be occupied. Benedict knew that his monks were men and that they should remain men. Everything, therefore, that pertained to the man should have its daily exercise. Prayer, praise, study, manual labor, were essential to wholesome human nature, the last quite as much as the other three.

Benedict's further directions showed him to be a man of almost uncanny common sense as well as of deep spiritual wisdom. Take one or two examples. First, his instructions to those who had charge of the utensils of the monastery—tools, plates, pots and pans, etc. The steward must be mature, wise, economical, not prodigal. He must care for the utensils of the monastery "as if they were the vessels of the altar." That is lofty counsel. It might to advantage be hung in a conspicuous place in many of our modern households, not only as an encouragement to honest work, but as a suggestion as to the dignity of household administration. Second, his regulations for the cooks. They were to go on duty every two weeks, an item which showed that nearly all the monks could cook. Whenever a cook took up his work he prostrated himself before the assembled monks, asked for their prayers and for the blessing of God in what he was about to undertake. At the end of his term he again prostrated himself before his brethren, and he asked God's blessing on what he had tried to do. It sounds a little quaint. But it was a good, a high-minded, rule. It helped to put the duties of the kitchen on a high plane. The spirit of the rule would not be amiss in our kitchens to-day. The cook may control not only the health, but also the temper, and consequently even the religion, of the household!

It was characteristic of Benedict that he touched nothing without giving it a quality of dignity. And he was peculiarly anxious that even those who came for the night should enter into the spirit of the Benedictine fellowship. The guest was to be cordially received and led at once to the abbot. The abbot would welcome him; together they would read the Bible and pray, and as long as the guest stayed under the roof of the monastery, he would eat his meals with the abbot. The guest was received as Christ would have been received.

The spirit of government, dictatorial though it seems to have been, was none the less lofty. It is true that the monk promised to obey, and that he abandoned his will to the abbot. But it was equally true that the abbot was not expected to come to an important decision without giving all the inmates of the monastery, *even the youngest*, an opportunity frankly to express their opinion. Then the abbot was to give the final judgment, reminding himself that he must render an account at the judgment seat of Christ. Yes, it was a dictatorship. But a dictatorship of this kind is near kin to the right kind of democracy. Given an abbot of pure heart and unselfish purpose, and men would be content with such leadership.

Such being the atmosphere of Monte Cassino, what kind of a daily programme did Benedict and his men pass through from the time they got out of bed until they got into it again? Their routine differed slightly with the changing seasons, but in general it was as follows.[11]

They got up at two o'clock in the morning. To some of us that seems a fairly early rising hour. However, whether that hour is early or not depends altogether upon the time one goes to bed. It is no more unreasonable to go to bed at six and rise at two, than it is to go to bed at two and rise at ten. It might even be discovered that the former were the better way, if a choice were to be made. It may be that some of the monks were awake and ready to rise even before the early bell

[11] *Benedictine Monachism*, chap. XVII, by E. Cuthbert Butler, gives the detailed routine for different seasons. I have given the programme for only one day and in somewhat general terms.

was rung. From two until half-past three they prayed. To those who either do not know how to pray or do not want to pray that regulation seems hard too. But some men know how to pray and like to do it. Many of these Benedictines probably looked forward to the hour of prayer. From half-past three to half-past four they gave themselves to meditation—a supreme satisfaction to those who had learned its joys. Again they prayed from half-past four until five. From five until nine they studied; they used their minds at definite mental tasks. At nine o'clock they were at their prayers again, as they were at approximately three-hour intervals for the rest of the day. From a quarter-past nine until noon and from the end of the noon-day service and siesta until four, they worked in the open air, in garden and field and about the monastery property. During their siesta they were free to sleep or to think or to read quietly until two o'clock—it was a siesta of more than an hour in addition to their nearly eight hours of sleep! At noon they had their single meal, at certain seasons having a second. Again the rule seems severe. The question arises, however, whether the critics are not over-eating! Compline came at about sunset followed by minor services. They were all in their beds in the big dormitories by half-past six. And to assure a quiet night Benedict sandwiched the young monks between those who were less eager for a frolic. Such was their programme. Summing it up,[12] they prayed and meditated for five and one-half hours; they read and studied for three and three-quarters hours; they worked with their hands for five and one-quarter hours; they ate and rested for nearly two hours; they slept for about seven hours and a half. It will be seen that not a moment was allowed for what we should call amusement or recreation. They got their exercise in field work rather than in games; like many a man outside a monastery they were contented with the diversion that came of praying, working, and sleeping in the companionship of those of like-minded purpose. Conversation, as such, was practically unknown, and it was unwanted. Necessary ideas only were to be imparted and those in the fewest words.

Such was the daily course of the men of Monte Cassino. Such the life they lived while the world outside was being torn to pieces, so that it might be remade in a better way. But, as I have said, the rule alone never would have gathered these men together, never would have kept them faithful and never would have made Monte Cassino an institution of such wholesome influence in the early Middle Ages had it not been that Benedict was there and that he had poured his personality into the rule. The Gospel is great because of

[12]E. Cuthbert Butler, *Benedictine Monachism,* p. 281.

Christ; the Benedictine Rule is great because of Benedict.

Gregory the Great was fully aware of this when he wrote the saint's life. He says little about the Rule, much about the man of whose spirit it was the child. And even though Gregory's story is filled with tales of wonder, many, possibly most, of which may be beyond our belief, yet it bears witness to a man of singular spirituality, possibly to a man whose powers were and are beyond the comprehension of the average mind. To attempt to discover the personality of Benedict within the unusual experiences told by Gregory may be a much surer way of finding it than by the method of first reducing the story to the character of a normal narrative. We must not forget that it was Benedict who was the interpreter of his own rule.[13] It was he who was with his men at prayer and praise and study and work. It was he who watched them when they were sick or when they were tempted or when they had yielded to temptation or had boldly fought their way through it. It was his love that breathed into the rule the breath of life. Let Gregory, then, tell us a few stories about Benedict and let us yield ourselves

[13]Cujus si quis velit subtilius mores vitamque cognoscere, potest in eadem institutione regulae omnes magisterii illius actus invenire: quia sanctus vir nullo modo potuit aliter docere quam vixit. *Vita.,* cap. XXXVI.

to the spiritual beauty that rests within their wonder.

Toward the end of Benedict's life Totila, the military chieftain of the Ostrogoths, was ravaging Italy. He had carried his campaign into the neighborhood of Monte Cassino. He had heard that Benedict "had the spirit of prophecy" and he wanted to put it to the test. Like Herod he hoped to see some miracle. Choosing one of his captains he clothed him in his own royal apparel and told him to go to Benedict feigning that he was the king. Benedict saw Riggo coming, and as soon as the captain was within earshot, he said to him, "Put off what thou wearest, it is not thine." Riggo fell to the ground in fear, and he and his men returned to Totila and told him how quickly they had been found out. Totila, himself, then ventured to approach. When he saw Benedict in the distance, seated, waiting for him, he too fell prostrate. And he would not rise until the good man came and raised him from the ground. Benedict rebuked Totila for his evil deeds. He told him that his future fate would be a punishment for his cruelty. In fear Totila withdrew down the mountain. "Never man spake like this man." Thereafter Totila was less cruel.

As Benedict was stern with the wrong-doer he was infinitely lovely with those who were pure in heart. And the serenity of his friendships, Gregory tells us, gave him experiences that few men have. One of Benedict's neighbors, Servandus, "like himself a man of heavenly grace," had come to visit him; they had talked together of the words of life and of the comforting food of the heavenly country and finally they had gone to their cells. Benedict did not sleep. He stood at his tower window and looked out into the darkness over the quiet valley of the Campagna and toward the hills beyond. Suddenly the darkness disappeared. It seemed as if the world were illuminated by one ray of the sun. As he beheld this marvel and wondered what it might mean he saw the soul of his friend Germanus, Bishop of Capua, carried by the angels to heaven, as it were in a sphere of flame. Twice and three times he called Servandus. Servandus came in time to see the last glow of the fading light. At once Benedict sent a messenger to Capua. The man returned and said that Germanus had died at the moment Benedict had had his heavenly vision.

St. Scholastica was Benedict's twin sister. We know hardly anything of her early life.[14] There is a strong tradition that she was among the first to respect her brother's decision to abandon the world and to go into seclusion. And it is said that she followed him to Subiaco and lived in her own

[14]Gregory, *Vita,* cap. XXXIII, says that she was dedicated to God from infancy.

cell not far from him. Whatever of truth there may be in these reports, it is quite certain that not long after Benedict and his monks built the monastery of Monte Cassino, St. Scholastica and women of similar purpose had a convent not far away. Brother and sister were spiritually in the deepest and most sensitive sympathy. But like the self-restrained men and women of those days they allowed themselves to see each other only once a year. Apparently they met on neutral ground. On the occasion of their last visit together they had given the whole day to the praise of God and to conversation about sacred things. As the night came on Scholastica asked her brother not to leave her but to spend the night talking about the joys of the heavenly life. "What are you talking about, sister," Benedict at once replied. "No, I cannot spend the night outside my cell." At the time the sky was clear, not a cloud was in sight. Hearing her brother's refusal, Scholastica buried her face in her hands and prayed. At once there was a terrific thunder-storm with floods of rain—so heavy that neither Benedict nor his men could think of venturing out. Turning to his sister, Benedict said, "May the all-powerful God spare thee, sister. What is this that thou hast done?" Scholastica answered, "I asked you and you would not listen to me. I asked God and He heard me." And so it came about that they spent the night in conversation about holy things. It was to be their last interview, for three days later as Benedict sat in his cell he raised his eyes toward the sky and he saw the soul of his sister in the form of a dove passing into the heavens. He rejoiced and praised God for his sister's happiness and he told the brethren that he himself had not long to live. He asked them to bring his sister's body to the monastery and he laid it in a tomb that he had made ready.

"And it came to pass that those whose minds were one in God were not to be separated in their burial."[15] As Benedict became aware that his time was short he told his friends and asked them to make ready for his end. On the day of his death the monks carried him into the chapel. He fortified his spirit with the Body and Blood of Christ. Supported in the arms of the monks the last breath passed from his body among the words of prayer.

On the same day two of the brothers, one in the monastery, the other far away, had the same vision. They saw as it were a carpet stretching from Benedict's cell into the heavens, and on either side of this pathway a row of lights, and one of venerable aspect, standing at the upper end, asked the brothers whether they knew the meaning of what they saw. They said that they did not.

[15]Gregory, *Vita,* cap. XXXIV.

He answered, "This is the way by which Benedict, the beloved of God, hath ascended into the heavens."

Such tales are not told of ordinary men.

## CHAPTER IV

## HILDEBRAND

After Benedict had died and after Pope Gregory I had written his life and had used the Benedictine monks in his missionary ventures Benedictine monasticism became a permanent factor in Western Church life. Not only did it direct the conduct of the individual who wanted to leave the city, retire into isolation, and give himself to prayer, contemplation, charity and study, but, in increasing numbers, it captured the cathedral clergy, reducing their life to a modified Benedictine Rule, and it became the basis of practically every monastic reform and of every new order. The personality of Benedict, as tradition preserved its power, and the singular common sense which every clause of the Rule expressed, were of contagious influence within the ministry of the Church. But they went, in their effect, far beyond the spheres of the monks and the cathedral clergy. The consequences of Benedictine monastic life and Benedictine monastic principles were to be discovered in the policies of some of the ablest of the Popes. Many of the noblest efforts of the mediæval papacy may be traced indirectly and directly to the movement Benedict set in motion.

Of all the Popes, Hildebrand was most monastically inclined, and of all the Popes he tried harder than any to secure to the Church certain of the monastic ideals. He may or he may not have been a monk; he may or he may not have been an inmate of the monastery at Cluny, but he was from beginning to end a monk at heart, and not even the abbots at Cluny worked harder than Hildebrand to achieve the Cluniac programme.

Hildebrand, or, as he is officially known, Pope Gregory VII, was born in about the year 1020. He died in the year 1085. When his days were numbered he said, "I have loved righteousness and hated iniquity, and therefore I die in exile." Apparently Hildebrand thought he had lived for a good cause, and that he was dying in consequence of the work he had done for it. He became Pope in the year 1073, and throughout the twelve years of his pontificate he had but one aim—to place the Church in a position of supremacy over the State, so that the Church might control the appointments to its own offices and thereby assure a ministry of sterling quality in positions that were both low and high. He met with defeat at the hands of the Emperor Henry IV, and therefore it may be said that he had died for a cause which at least he himself thought great. Without question the cause was not only great, but it was of vital necessity for the times in which Hildebrand lived. Society at that period was built upon a feudal foundation. Christianity was, so far as the West was concerned, built upon a Papal foundation. It was inevitable, therefore, that Popes should conceive of Papal supremacy in feudal terms, and feudal terms demanded that the Church should be superior to the State if it wished to control the religious situation.

It is impossible, however, thoroughly to understand the cause for which Hildebrand fought and the contribution which he made unless one appreciates the quality of influence that the Papacy had already achieved.

Centuries before Hildebrand's day the Roman Church had inherited the imperial traditions of the Roman State. When Constantine in 323 had left Rome and had transferred the seat of Empire to Constantinople, he had been compelled to leave the imperial traditions behind. He might take with him his records and his officials and his armies, but the millennium-long traditions could not be moved. They remained in the West. They became the property of the institution whose centre was there; they increased the prestige of that institution's head. The Roman Church was the beneficiary. The Bishop of Rome gathered about himself the imperial character.

In past generations the Roman Church had achieved a reputation for common sense. When in the second century various sections of the Church were observing Easter on either the Sunday or the day of the week that commended itself to them, and for which there seemed to be Biblical warrant, Rome demanded that there be a date common to all. Most of the Church saw the point and conformed to Roman custom. When in the third and fourth centuries the rigorists—Novationists and Donatists—were declaring that those who had fallen from the faith, either through sacrificing to the genius of the Emperor, or through surrendering the Scriptures into the hands of the persecutors, should not be allowed to return into communion, the Church at Rome said that on sign of true repentance they should be reinstated. Later, the Church at large agreed. When in the third century many were protesting that baptism by heretical clergy should not be thought valid, Rome replied that all baptism was valid when performed in the name of the Father, the Son and the Holy Ghost. The general Church accepted the decision.

The Roman Church from very early days had a genius for religious experience and statement. Representing the whole of the West, and speaking through Pope Leo I (440–461), it expressed the faith of both East and West at the Council of

Chalcedon in 451. While the East was still in doubt about the nature of the person of Christ, Rome spoke clearly and wisely, and her decision has been widely accepted from that day to this.

The Roman Church was conscious of the "burden of all the Churches." Gregory I (590–604), statesman, scholar, missionary, secured to the Anglo-Saxons the Christian religion. His sending Augustine and his encouraging him with excellent advice were only an example of his advisory relation with others of the Western Churches. The young nations of the West recognized his purpose and acknowledged his spiritual supremacy. To mention Rome in the days of Gregory was to suggest an interest of a helpful and broad-minded character.

The Roman Church was unselfishly determined upon, and enthusiastically eager for, unity of East and West, and for a centralization of power in the Bishop of Rome. Nicholas I (858–867) in a high-minded and statesmanlike way made overtures to Constantinople, realizing that a divided Church must of necessity be weak. And he naïvely, although in good faith, took advantage of the Pseudo-Isidorean Decretals. Although certain of the bishops of France had possibly forged this curious document to rid themselves of obedience to their immediate superiors—the archbishops and patriarchs, Nicholas looked upon it as a genuine and ancient support of the Papal supremacy. And he used his authority for the good of the Church as he understood it.

Hitherto, on the whole, the Papacy had achieved a position of prominence in direct proportion to its deserts. It had manifested common sense, sagacity, and religion. It was entitled to a place of supreme power. At the beginning of the tenth century, however, the election to the Papacy fell into the hands of the political factions of the central part of Italy, and, in consequence, was used as an instrument by which either party strove to gain supreme control in Roman civic affairs. In fact, it is quite certain that for a generation or more two notorious women had the virtual naming of the Popes. Christendom was shocked, and the conscience of the Church itself became sensitive to the point of determining upon vigorous action. The Emperor, Otto I, marched down upon Rome, and cleansed the frightful Augean stables.

For a time the condition of the Papacy improved, but only for a time, for in the beginning of the eleventh century there was a recurrence of the same situation owing to a similar cause. Politics assumed control, and the Papacy suffered. In the year 1046 the Emperor Henry III marched into Rome, and, at the Synod of Sutri, deposed the three contending Popes. It was a work of necessity. The atmosphere was temporarily cleared. The regeneration of the Papacy had begun.

Again, before one can fully understand the character of the programme which was introduced into Papal affairs in the middle of the eleventh century, it is necessary to survey briefly the political situation in the West. To imagine that Europe was at that time divided into nations much as it is to-day would be altogether to misconceive the situation. The German Empire was with great difficulty kept together. It consisted of a large number of loosely federated sections, the federation itself depending almost altogether upon the power of the reigning Emperor. France was hardly more than a collection of territories over which powerful war-lords held their sway, the king being only slightly more powerful than any of his feudal adherents. In the ninth century the Norman marauders had penetrated the heart of France by means of the rivers, and had gradually secured a firm footing in the section of France which we now call Normandy. They had also, at a later date, sailed into the Mediterranean and secured a position in Sicily and in the southern part of Italy. England in the days immediately prior to the Norman conquest hardly deserved the name of a nation. The land was filled with barons, each controlling the section over which he held hereditary sway, and each allied to the king only when his own interests and the general welfare of England were concerned. The days of the Danish invasion were not far in the past, and the days of the assimilation of the Danes were of very recent date. It is readily seen, therefore, that the Papacy had not to deal with sections of the West which were conscious of their national unity, but rather with parts of the world in which a very crude nationality was beginning to appear. The conception of law upon which these kingdoms were based was of the most rudimentary order, judgment by ordeal frequently taking the place of judgment according to due process of law. The Canon Law, in its systematic arrangement and in its adaptation to complicated problems, was infinitely superior to the crude legal systems of the young nations. It was evident, therefore, that unless there were to be unbridled nationalism and royal will uncontrolled by responsibility to a higher power, Western Europe would shortly be in a condition of anarchy.

The position in which the Papacy found itself by the middle of the eleventh century was rendered somewhat more acute by the imperial insistence that Popes should be elected only on the virtual nomination or consent of the Emperors themselves. Whereas the interference of Emperors like Otto I and Henry III was of distinct advantage to the Papacy, the principle upon which their power rested was of an insidious and dangerous kind. In effect it meant that although the Papacy had been pulled out of local Italian politics by the strong hands of the Emperors, it was likely again to be plunged into imperial politics in consequence of the Emperors' helpful interference.

At this moment a movement became operative in Italy the purpose of which was to separate completely the Church from the State, so that the Church might carry on its spiritual work unhampered by political entanglements. This movement had its rise in the monastery of Cluny; it was espoused only gradually by the Papal party itself. In the year 910 William of Aquitaine had given to the abbot and the monks of Cluny the buildings in which they lived, and the property upon which the buildings stood. His purpose, apparently, was to rid the monastery of possible complications with landlords who might not have as lofty a conception of the monastic life as he himself had cherished. The consequence of this gift was probably unforeseen by William. As time went on, however, it was evident to all that in giving the property to the monks themselves, he had virtually made a gift of the monastic lands and buildings to the Papacy, for after the transfer the abbot and his monks owed their allegiance (although at first it was a spiritual allegiance only)

THE ABBEY CHURCH OF CLUNY

From an engraving after the drawing by Lallemand of Dijon, dated 1787

directly to the Popes rather than directly to the local princes.

Cluny was true to the genius of its foundation, for out of the monastery there came a policy of a threefold nature which was destined to give the Popes a position not only of practical independence of the State, but also of superiority to it.

The first item of the threefold programme was that lay princes should not have power to invest the clergy with the insignia of their office. The clergy of the day had a double capacity. They were at once officials of the Church and officials of the State. It was thought necessary that the local prince should have supreme control of all men who were the immediate lords of landed estates, either large or small. The military necessity of this rule is obvious. On the other hand, however, it is equally obvious that the Church ran great danger of having its bishops, abbots, and even its parish priests, chosen from those men who were likely best to serve the local prince's interests. The danger, therefore, was acute that in the vast majority of cases politics would stand first and religion second. Such, in fact, was the widespread result of this system. The monastery of Cluny saw the critical nature of the situation; it sought its remedy in the removal of the ecclesiastic from any contact with the local prince. Thereafter the bishop, for example, should be invested with his insignia only by a representative of the Church, and in consequence should be considered primarily the Church's man. Assuming that the motive of the Church was good, the endeavor on the part of Cluny was excellent.

Cluny's second attempt was to make it impossible for any of the clergy to buy their positions. One of the crying evils of the time was the sale of bishoprics, abbacies and lesser positions to the highest bidder,[1] and the consequent imperfect despatch of the Church's spiritual work. In many cases the man in possession of the benefice would take the income from his lands and engage as his substitute a man who would but imperfectly care for the spiritual welfare of the benefice, while he himself enjoyed the income elsewhere. Cluny therefore was quite right in saying that no one should receive an ecclesiastical appointment if he were suspected of simony, and that no one should remain in office if he were guilty of simony. Poor old Simon Magus! He never would have offered Peter money for the gift of the Holy Ghost if he had known that his mistake would be remembered so long!

Thirdly, Cluny sought to have all the clergy of the Church unmarried men. The custom of a celibate clergy, although dating back to a very early period in the Church, was by no means uni-

[1]Commonly called simony.

versal as late as the middle of the tenth century. In fact, another century was to go by before the Western Church in general was to commit itself to the idea. The motive of Cluny in this respect is not so clear as that in regard to the other two planks in the platform. It is obvious that Cluny looked on the unmarried state as the higher spiritual condition. Beyond this, however, it is almost equally obvious that Cluny had an economic purpose. If, for example, the clergy were to be married while in many instances holding vast estates, the desire to bequeath their property to their children would be strong, and in consequence the clergy themselves would be absorbed in secular matters while their primary interest ought to lie in affairs of a spiritual character. Certain notorious instances connected with the Papacy of a later date as well as of times contemporary with Cluny make this inference quite clear. It had been proved that the temptation to win, to control and to hold ecclesiastical property was almost irresistible.

Such was the threefold programme emanating from the monastery of Cluny. For about 150 years the Cluniac ideal was gradually getting under way, and by the middle of the eleventh century it had been espoused in Rome as the most hopeful platform upon which to base the policy of Church reform.

Along with the programme of Cluny there went another movement which was destined in the long run to confine the election of the Popes to the Church alone. I mean the foundation of the College of Cardinals. In the year 1059 Pope Nicholas II issued a law confining the election of Popes to the seven cardinal bishops in the neighborhood of Rome. Thereafter they alone were to elect the Pope, although after the election they were to notify the Emperor of their choice. The immediate effect of this election-law was not to secure the full purpose of the law itself, for it was difficult to divorce the Emperor from very close connection with the Papal choice. However, the ideal was expressed, and an earnest demand was made to realize it. In the pontificate of Alexander III, about 125 years later, cardinal-presbyters and cardinal-deacons were added to the cardinal bishops, and the College of Cardinals, as it is formed virtually at the present day, was brought into existence. It is important to notice not so much the practical working out of this attempt as the ideal which underlay it. Again, like the programme of Cluny, it sought to separate entirely the affairs of the Church from the affairs of the State, so that the Gospel might be truly preached, and so that the care of souls might be entrusted to men unentangled with the affairs of the world.

It is at this juncture that Hildebrand appears

as an active member of the Papal group. He becomes, as it were, a power behind the throne, in the middle of the century, and remains such with increasing influence until he himself accepts the election to the Papacy.

Hildebrand was born in the little Tuscan village of Sovana, in a very picturesque part of the country. His father and mother were people of humble position. When he was fifteen years of age he went to Rome to continue his education, and there he became connected with the monastery of St. Mary on the Aventine. His uncle, who was closely associated with the monastery, watched the boy with interest and enthusiasm. One of Hildebrand's teachers was John Gratian, who later became Pope Gregory VI.

Early in his twenties Hildebrand showed signs of singular executive ability. His powers were noticed by the contemporary Pope, who gave him important work within the charitable regions of Rome. From this he succeeded to the position of archdeacon. In those days the work of the archdeacon was primarily of a spiritual character. It later had to do with the business affairs of the Papal possessions in the heart of Italy. Such work, however, brought Hildebrand into the closest contact with the contemporary Popes. His former teacher, John Gratian, as I have said, had become Pope Gregory VI. Gratian had bought the office from a good motive. He wanted to win the Papal chair and to convert it into an agency for good. The only method open to him was to commit the sin of simony. He bought the Papacy. He did wrong that right might come. When Henry III came down from Germany and deposed the three contending Popes in the year 1046, Gregory VI, with the other Popes, had to leave Rome. Hildebrand, his close friend and former pupil, went with him into exile. Gregory, more of a saint than a statesman, died in Germany shortly afterward. Hildebrand returned to Rome in the company of Bruno of Toul, who later was to become Pope Leo IX. Bruno's entry into Rome must have been impressive, and also prophetic of the policy he was about to follow. He entered the Eternal City barefoot, and announced to the citizens of Rome that he would not accept the Papal office unless they and the bishops elected him and unless they were willing to follow his lead in purifying the Church in head and members. His comparatively brief term of office was the strong beginning of the attempt to embody the Cluniac ideal.

Hildebrand was not particularly conspicuous during these years. He was, however, gaining rapidly in power, and when one comes to the Papacy of Alexander II, one finds Hildebrand exercising a very potent influence. Alexander II stood for the strong Cluniac programme. He also secured his political position by trying to make peace with the Normans in the South, who were constantly gaining in strength, and with the peoples of the North who were democratically inclined, and who were ready to fight for a purified Church. For these things Hildebrand himself had stood valiantly, and was later to press with extraordinary vigor. Alexander died in the year 1073. While his funeral services were going on, a cry went up, "Hildebrand for Pope!" The call was unanimous. In fact, it was irresistible. And Hildebrand accepted the election, although it took place in this extraordinary, irregular manner—a manner, superficially at least, in direct contradiction to the law of 1059 which had founded the College of Cardinals, a law the purpose of which was to separate the affairs of the Church from the affairs of the State, and a law behind which Hildebrand himself had taken his position. However, one of the most hopeful aspects of the interpretation of the canon law is that common sense is superior to the letter of the law itself. Hildebrand undoubtedly knew that he was accepting an irregular, even though valid, election. He also knew that he alone could assume power at that particular moment with a promise of carrying through the critical programme of Cluny and of his own predecessors; and it is interesting to note that not until he got into troubles of a totally different nature was this fact introduced into the charges brought against him.

For so forceful a man Hildebrand had few of the usual marks of greatness. He was conspicuous in nothing physically except possibly in his penetrating glance. He was not large; his voice was not strong. Although he was able in debate he was in no sense a scholar. He was undoubtedly familiar with much of the canon law, but he does not rank with the canon lawyers. His greatness lies rather in the depth of his convictions and in his tenacity of purpose to carry them through to victory. That the bulk of his labors found its fulfilment in the accomplishments of Popes who, in many ways, were abler than he, is evidence enough that he possessed abilities of a high order.

As if he were passing official opinion on the status of his old teacher, John Gratian, deposed by Henry III, Hildebrand took the name of Gregory VII. At once he started with vigor upon his programme of reform. In many a council in the City of Rome he reviewed the situation of the Church and saw to it that laws were passed regulating the lives of the clergy and securing proper appointments to ecclesiastical offices. Immediately also his programme brought him into critical contact with the nations of the West. I shall not speak of these instances in their chronological order, but rather in the sequence of their relative importance.

Philip I of France had been appointing bishops to offices for which they were not spiritually qualified. Hildebrand wrote to the French bishops and asked that these affairs might be taken up in council, and that the king might be reminded of the nature of his conduct. The French bishops were loath to come into irritating contact with their sovereign. The sovereign himself persisted in his former policy. After repeatedly urging the bishops of France to do their part, Gregory wrote that if the king would not mend his ways, he himself would go to France and snatch the kingdom from his hands. It was an extraordinary threat, even for those days. It was a most undiplomatic communication to send to a king. It was impossible of practical fulfilment. On the other hand, its purpose must be noted, and Hildebrand must be judged not so much according to the principles of policy or of practicability, but according to his intention. He was confident that there should be a power superior to kings, to which kings themselves should be responsible, and that only in the realization of this close connection between kings and Popes, the Pope being the king's spiritual superior, could the welfare of national churches be secured.

Hildebrand's relation with England was of a

somewhat more genial order, but its character was none the less definite. When William the Conqueror went over into England and defeated the English at Hastings in 1066, he carried with him the Papal banners. They were a gift of Pope Alexander II to the Norman army. Without any doubt the Pope thought that the receiving of these banners was an acknowledgment that the invading armies were nothing more or less than the crusading host of the Pope. They were to go into England under the Papal blessing. They were to conquer the somewhat disorderly Anglo-Saxon people, and they were to secure a closer alliance between England and Rome. Without any question also, William the Conqueror's view was somewhat different. Hildebrand wrote to William and asked him to recognize Rome as England's feudal superior. William responded with dignity and also with finality. He said: "Fealty I have refused to offer, nor will I; for I neither promised it nor do I find that my predecessors did it to your predecessors." And the affair was apparently closed. Furthermore, William enacted certain laws which determined the relation of the English to the Papacy. He said that no clergy were to leave England to visit Rome without the royal leave; that no excommunications from Rome should become operative in England without the royal permission; that no Papal bulls should be published in England without the king's consent; and that no cases that might be tried in the courts of England should be tried in the courts of Rome without the king's approval. In other words, there was to be a royal check on intercourse with Rome and with the Pope. It is needless to add that William never dreamed of touching the details of the faith. In fact he was a most loyal defender of the points of view for which Rome stood. He himself had introduced into England the system of ecclesiastical courts, and under the direction of his archbishop, Lanfranc, the courts were working to the satisfaction of both Church and State. It is noticeable that Hildebrand writes letters of a firm but cautious character to the Archbishop of Canterbury, and although he is eager to have a closer association between England and Rome, he apparently thinks that the internal affairs of the British Isles are being so well taken care of by William and his high-minded archbishop that he had better let well-enough alone.

However, even if Hildebrand had wanted to press to a favorable solution the problems connected with Papal supremacy in France and England, he could not do so, for the much more critical difficulty of the relationship of the Pope to the German King was demanding his almost exclusive attention.

The good Emperor Henry III had died in 1056.

His son Henry was elected king in his stead. Henry IV had come to the throne at six years of age. He had evidently not been properly trained during the long and weak regency of his mother. The possession of power had strengthened his will rather than his character. When Hildebrand became Pope in 1073 Henry was only twenty-three years old. Henry had already surrounded himself with unprincipled and excommunicated advisers, and he had not hesitated to exercise his royal power in making appointments to bishoprics. Both of these acts of his ran counter to the programme laid down by Cluny and supported by Hildebrand and his immediate predecessors. Hildebrand wrote to Henry in a paternal and friendly way urging him to turn to other advisers and to refrain from ecclesiastical appointments. As the king was waging war against the Saxons, and therefore could not afford to enlarge the number of his enemies, he made at least an appearance of yielding to the Pope's advice. But after the Saxons had been conquered and Henry felt himself to be more securely seated on his throne, he returned to his old habits. Hildebrand again urged him to mend his ways, threatening him with excommunication if he did not follow the Papal counsel. The king imagined himself strong enough to do as he pleased, and he scorned the counsel of one who, although exercising a more searching power than any Pope before him, was eager to be the king's friend.

The controversy had raised the question of the limits of royal and Papal authority—a question that was not to be settled for another fifty years. As for the king, he was determined to be master of the German Church as well as of the German State. At the mere request of a Pope, even though the Pope were supported by the century-long ideal of Cluny that the State should at no point come in contact with the Church, Henry did not purpose to surrender his control over men who were masters not only of souls, but of vast territorial domains. If Henry had been a more high-minded man; if, like William the Conqueror, he had seemed to have the spiritual welfare of his State at heart—he might have resisted Hildebrand with determination and with dignity. Instead, however, he lost his temper, called a council at Worms, spoke of the Pope with contempt, and had sentence of deposition passed against him by a body wholly incompetent to take such action. The battle had begun.

Henry now proceeded to wage the war in the enemy's camp. He wrote to Hildebrand addressing the letter "Henry, not by usurpation but by God's holy will, King, to Hildebrand, not Pope, but false monk." And he brought the letter to the following climax: "Descend from the apostolic throne which thou hast usurped, that another may take it, who will not do violence to religion, but will teach the true doctrine of Peter. I, Henry, by God's grace King, with all our bishops call on thee: Descend, descend." Not contented with a letter only, a priest named Roland was sent to Rome to announce the decree, and Henry, as Patrician of Rome, called upon the Romans to put the decree into execution. Roland entered the Lateran council and at once called upon the Pope "to descend," and upon the bishops to assemble with the king to elect another Pope. At once the measure of Roman respect for the Papacy was manifest. It was with difficulty that Roland escaped with his life.

At the same council the king was excommunicated. Hildebrand went even further: he declared that Henry had forfeited the crown and that his subjects were released from their allegiance. In these modern days of diversity of opinion on religious matters and of separation of Church and State, we cannot picture the situation. It was as if a monarch were deprived of office because of insanity, for to be of bad report in the Church was equivalent to being thought of unsound mind. The king was shocked and terrified. He knew that his frontier enemies would take advantage of the occasion to gain their end; he saw his princes and his bishops falling away from him; he feared that another king might be elected in his stead.

Henry, therefore, took the first step toward reconciliation. His princes had told him that they would choose a successor if his excommunication were not removed at the end of a year. They had already called a council at Augsburg to discuss the baffling situation. They had asked the Pope to attend it. And the Pope was on his way. Henry, however, knowing that he, as an excommunicated man, would be at a disadvantage in the council, determined first to secure absolution. He set out to meet Hildebrand.

The Pope had begun his northward journey, but, fearing treachery, he had gone to Canossa, there to await the royal escort that was to conduct him into Germany. Canossa was a castle boldly situated on the estates of the Countess Matilda, a woman of almost royal possessions and power. At present there is hardly a trace of Canossa left. In those days, however, it was an imposing fortress, commanding a view to the southeast along the summits of the highest of the Apennines and to the north across the wide valley of the Po. Within this castle Hildebrand awaited his escort. Friends of Henry had preceded him. They pleaded with the Pope for mercy. Even the Abbot of Cluny asked Hildebrand to be lenient. And although Matilda herself urged Hildebrand to see the penitent, the Pope kept the king standing before the gate for three days. One report tells us that he stood there in the snow, barefoot, clad as a penitent. At last the king was admitted. The Pope absolved him on condition that he would surrender the crown into the Pope's hands, become a private individual until a council might pass on his case, and swear obedience to the Pope. The king consented. Gregory then celebrated Mass. After he had consecrated the elements, he said, "If I am guilty of the offences laid to my charge, may the tasting of this wafer be my instant death." He turned to Henry and challenged him to do likewise. Henry, perhaps with shame, perhaps at last in a manly way, declined to meet the test.

The victory might have been entirely with Hildebrand had he been contented with his progress and had he not pressed his advantage beyond the point of German endurance. The disaffected princes had elected a counter-king in the person of Rudolph of Swabia. Rudolph had been temporarily successful against Henry. Hildebrand unwisely supported the cause of Rudolph. The Pope's motive was doubtless good. He saw that Henry had returned to his old ways and that he had gone back to his old advisers. He wanted a king who would support the Papal policy. But in order to protect the Church he ran the great risk of entering too intimately into the affairs of the State. A second time he excommunicated and deposed the king. At once the offended nationalism of Germany began to assert itself.

Henry, now strongly supported by princes and bishops, determined to retaliate. He called a council which, more seriously than the first, deposed Hildebrand and named Guibert of Ravenna as anti-Pope. He forced the conflict into Rome itself, encouraged the desertion of many of the cardinals and finally saw Guibert seated in St. Peter's chair as Clement III. Hildebrand had overshot the mark. He had been impatient and undiplomatic. His cause was one of the best; the means he chose by which to win his purpose were the only ones at hand—the feudal supremacy of the Church. But he forgot that there was such a thing as national consciousness; he did not realize that the people could not be expected to perceive the character of his contention as clearly as he himself did. A Pope in the right was being perhaps rightly defeated by a king in the wrong. When Henry entered and took the Leonine city, Hildebrand was forced to take refuge in the Castle of St. Angelo. Henry even then attempted to bargain with the stubborn defenders of Rome and with Hildebrand for the surrender of Rome, even offering to receive the imperial crown from the hands of Hildebrand. The Romans would have had Hildebrand yield. But the Pope preferred that the city should be destroyed and that he himself should be driven away rather than that he should seem to sanction wrong.

Two events now took place, the consequences of which were the exile and death of Hildebrand. The Romans were exhausted with the endless struggle; they thought that Hildebrand could bring it to a peaceful issue if he chose to do so; they turned from him to Henry. Robert Guiscard, the king of the south Italian Normans, not so much in love with Hildebrand as hostile to Henry, offered Hildebrand his protection. He might have come earlier to the rescue if he had cared to do so. He might possibly have saved Rome to Hildebrand and the diminishing group of those who understood the Pope's purpose. At length he came, sacked the city ruthlessly and involved Hildebrand in the hatred that the Romans should have limited to Guiscard alone. True, Hildebrand had appealed to Robert, and Robert had come with the Pope's blessing, and so he seemed to the people to be guiltily involved in the destruction of the city. But Hildebrand's motive was pure while Robert's was base.

When the Normans withdrew to the south, Hildebrand went with them. After twelve years of devotion to his purpose, he followed the army to Salerno, and there, about a year later, he breathed his last. He was still unconquered in spirit; he still knew that Henry was wrong and that he himself was right; he still thought that Rome should be supreme in spite of the fact that the city lay in ashes; he still was confident that for the welfare of Europe, for the victory of morals and religion, the Church should be wholly free from the State; until the end he was convinced that if the Church were to attain its purpose Popes must be superior to kings.

It is said that his last words were, "I have loved righteousness and hated iniquity, and therefore I die in exile." Whether or not these words were literally uttered by Hildebrand, they are a perfect description of his own conception of his life's work. His own private life was above suspicion. He lived as he taught. From the beginning of his career in Rome he had warmly espoused the programme of the Monastery of Cluny. If he believed that no priest should receive office at the hands of a prince, he had worked hard and unselfishly to persuade priest and prince and he had tried to set the example. If he thought that the clergy should not marry he not only never dreamed of marriage for himself, but he worked unceasingly in Italy and throughout Europe to establish celibacy. If he was persuaded that the close association of politics and religion was sapping the vitality of the Church, before he was Pope he had supported every measure leading to their separation, and during his rule he had made no compromise. He had not only dealt with the local Roman situation; he had struggled with kings. As he conceived righteousness he had loved it; as he understood iniquity he had hated it.

And yet he died in exile. It was inevitable that he should. The Europe of his day could not understand the fundamentally useful nature of his contention. Ecclesiastics who were princes and soldiers could with difficulty understand why Hildebrand should try to make them responsible only to him. Kings who depended upon the assistance that might be given them by their subjects who lived on episcopal and monastic lands could hardly comprehend why he should allow no royal check upon appointments to spiritual offices. In fact kings might with justice reply that Popes as well as kings had taken advantage of their power. Furthermore, in his zeal for the full realization of his purpose he had probably overlooked the fact of which William the Conqueror had so forcefully reminded him: he had forgotten that the young nations might possibly welcome such a Papal control as would leave them free to take care of their own internal affairs. The ideas of nationalism and internationalism must be allowed to develop side by side. Very pardonably Hildebrand lost sight of this. His zeal had eaten him up. Therefore he died in exile.

Almost immediately after his death, however, Western Europe seemed in a measure to accept his conception of society. In 1095 Urban II preached a crusade. The young nations took the cross and went to the Holy Land under the banners of a West united under the Papacy. In 1106 Henry I of England agreed that thereafter the king should not invest ecclesiastics with the insignia of their spiritual office. Kings would retain only investiture with the sceptre, the sign of their temporal power. It was a compromise, but it carried much of Hildebrand's principle. The Empire itself accepted a similar compromise at Worms in 1122. In 1215 representatives of the Western Church gathered at the Fourth Lateran council and declared the Pope to be the Prince of Princes. And even England, which wisely and strongly protested against the action of King John when he laid his crown at the feet of the legate of Pope Innocent III to receive it again as a gift from his feudal superior, was immensely comforted when Papal legates assisted in the government of England during the minority of John's son Henry. Hildebrand was stubborn, undiplomatic, impatient. But he had hold of an eternal principle. If morality and religion were to prosper, there must be an international check upon the nations.

## CHAPTER V

### FRANCIS OF ASSISI

St. Francis was born in the year 1182. He died in the year 1226. In 1228 Pope Gregory IX made Francis a saint of the Church. The poet Dante, who was born in 1265 and who wrote *The Divine Comedy* about seventy-five years after Francis died, placed the saint in the highest circle of heaven along with St. Augustine and St. Benedict.[1] Such was the opinion of Francis held by his contemporaries and by those living shortly after his own day.

The remarkable life upon which his contemporary reputation rested and upon which his constantly increasing influence is based fell between the years 1205 and 1226. In this brief space he lived the life and did the work which has given him a position in the spiritual history of the West inferior only to that of our Lord.

Half of these years fall within the period during which Innocent III was Pope of Rome and when the Church was in danger of yielding to the tendency of over-organization. Because of the Papacy's great success in gaining the control of society, in order that the Church might be free

[1] *Paradise,* XXXII.

*Photo, Alinari.*

ST. FRANCIS AND SOME OF THE SCENES IN HIS LIFE

from political entanglement, the Church might forget its mission. Francis saw the danger, and, for a while at least, seemed successfully to check it. He met the emphasis of over-organization with the emphasis of the spiritual life.

Pope Innocent III had in great measure realized the ambition of Hildebrand. He had, in a very real way, made the Church feudally superior to the State. Innocent amply deserved his position of supremacy. Measuring him by the standards of his day he was a man of integrity and ability. He was intelligent and well-informed. His character was above suspicion. He stood high in rank among the canon lawyers of his time. And the dowager empress apparently was proud to have him the guardian of her son, later the Emperor Frederick II. Furthermore, Innocent proved himself to be of singularly forceful character by bringing to their maturity certain important movements of the day. Under his leadership the Twelfth Ecumenical Council, in 1215, defined the doctrine of Transubstantiation. Henceforth the faithful were to believe that after the words of consecration had been uttered by the priest, the bread and wine were mere accidents while the Body and Blood of Christ were present in their stead. Under his inspiration and in the same council the Pope was declared to be the Prince of Princes. Henceforth the faithful were to recognize that there was a power superior to kings and emperors and that the Church for purposes of morals and religion was above the State.

While Innocent was engaged in achieving his unselfish ambition, he, like Hildebrand, came in contact, and, in some instances, in conflict with the nations of the West. With his lofty standard of international morality it was inevitable that he should. Fully conscious of his position of moral and religious responsibility he did not hesitate to pursue the policy he thought right whether it entailed the friendship or the enmity of the nations. The kingdom of Aragon was conspicuous among those many nations which peacefully yielded to the Papal claim. King Peter went to Rome, laid his crown on the altar of the Papal Church and received it again at the hands of the Pope as a feudal gift. The kingdom of France, on the contrary, was among those the monarchs of which reluctantly assented to the Pope's control. King Philip II had married Ingeborg of Denmark. After many years of married life he had wearied of her and had finally divorced her and had married Agnes of Meran. In clear-cut and final terms Innocent commanded Philip to dismiss Agnes and to take back his first wife. Outwardly at least the King obeyed.

Innocent was to have a more turbulent time with England. King John, the monarch who shares with William Rufus the reputation of being the vilest man who ever wore the English crown, was on the throne. The quarrel between king and Pope had to do with the election of an archbishop of Canterbury. The monks of Canterbury had met and had duly elected their man. The king, angered by their independent choice, and eager to have a tool of his own in a position of such commanding political as well as religious importance, repudiated their nominee and named another. Both parties appealed to the Pope. Innocent, wisely, but possibly somewhat beyond the letter of his legal rights, refused to consent to the election of either and pressed the election of Stephen Lancton, later to prove himself to be one of the ablest men who ever sat in Augustine's chair at Canterbury. The monks obediently followed the Pope's suggestion. At this John fell into a passionate fit of anger. He repudiated the joint selection of monks and Pope. And, strange to say, in doing so he was altogether within the letter of his rights, for no one might be elected either bishop or archbishop without the royal consent. It will shortly be seen, however, that he was not within the spirit of his rights, for it was assumed that in the appointment to Canterbury the king would have the religious interests of the kingdom at heart. John refused to allow Lancton to enter England.

Innocent, knowing that his own choice was good and that the king's was likely to be bad, retaliated with the terrific weapon of the interdict, or, in other words, with an excommunication of the entire kingdom. It meant that until John might repent there should be neither baptisms nor confirmations, nor communions, nor marriages, nor burials in consecrated ground. And although it also meant that England's clergy would, as usual, exercise their common sense and make occasional exceptions to the Pope's command, still the inconvenience was great, the spiritual dissatisfaction profound, the consciousness that the king was in some way in the wrong widespread. The nation was a spiritual outlaw not only in the eyes of the Pope but also in the opinion of the nations of the West; God and the kingdom were at variance. Nevertheless the king did not yield.

When Innocent saw that John was not to be brought to a better mind by such methods as these he declared him deposed; he asked Philip II of France to carry the sentence into effect, and to place his own son Louis on the English throne. At last John realized that the Pope was in earnest, for not only did he know that the Head of the Church was his foe, but he saw his barons falling away from him and he became more vividly aware of the growing hostility of his subjects. He stood alone. Only then he came to himself, and, quite characteristically, he selfishly caught at the only means of self-preservation. He jumped to the opposite extreme. He went to Dover, met the Pope's legate, laid the English crown at his feet and received it again from the legate's hands as a gift from the Church. The king was now reconciled to his superior; the interdict was raised. England again enjoyed its full religious privileges.

However, John escaped from one difficulty only to become involved in another. Now that he was the Pope's man the barons were determined that they should secure their rights against both king and Pope. They gathered on the island of Runnymede, not far from Windsor, and there they forced the reluctant king to sign the Great Charter, by the terms of which the barons and those whom they represented were thereafter to have their rights secured over against the encroachments of both king and Pope. And as a sign that a very essential and high-minded purpose inspired the authors and champions of the charter, it is interesting to note that Stephen Lancton, an Englishman, the Pope's own appointee to Canterbury, was the leader and spokesman of the barons. Again there was a conflict, not between two parties, one of which was altogether right and the other altogether wrong, but between two parties both of which were at least partially right. The barons were right in asserting England's privilege to control its own internal affairs. The Pope was right in insisting upon the principle that kings were subject to a moral and religious power higher than themselves.

My only purpose in referring to these national incidents in general and to the strife with England in particular is to show in what danger the Popes were, even the best of them, of being lost in the detail of controversy and of trying to gain their ends by methods that might conceal the spirit that inspired their claims. The quieter phases of the spiritual life were likely either to be lost from view or to fall into a place of secondary importance. Even to some of the most discerning men of the time it seemed as if ecclesiastical politics were the sole interest of the Church.

While such problems as these were occupying the time and mind of Innocent he dreamed a dream. On the preceding day, according to his custom, he had been taking his daily exercise in the cloisters of St. John Lateran. Possibly he was thinking of France and England and of the moral and religious ideal for which he would have them stand. He suddenly became aware of some one approaching. He raised his eyes and there before him stood a beggar, clothed in rags. Fearing that the stranger meant mischief, Innocent withdrew within the palace. As he slept that night he dreamed that the walls of the Lateran were about to fall, and that they would have fallen had not that same beggar, thin, in rags, but of lovely face, leaned up against the walls and held them in their place. It was Francis who was to save the Church. It was the life of self-sacrifice that was to bind the nations together.

Francis came at a time when men were hungering for the life of the spirit. It must not be thought that he was alone either in his purpose or in his accomplishment. He was unique only in that he was the greatest spiritual genius of his day. There were other individuals warning the Church and the clergy against too great conformity to the world; there were movements of a distinctly spiritual nature which showed that nothing but religion would suffice.

While Francis was a boy, Joachim of Floris, a strange religious enthusiast, possibly a fanatic, was going about appealing to clergy and people. He tried to recall the Church to the heart of its mission. He said, "The Church can and could retire into solitude, lead a spiritual life, abide in communion with Christ her Bridegroom; and through her love for Him she would become mistress of the world, and perhaps no longer be subject to pay quitrent."[2] St. Hildegarde gave very

[2]Neander, *Hist. of Christian Religion and Church,* ed. 1851, VII, 301.

homely counsel to those who came to urge her to influence the will of God in their favor, "Because you have besought me, I will beseech God for you; but let Him do what, according to His grace and mercy, He has determined to do."[3] Furthermore, she boldly arraigned the clergy for hasty or careless excommunication; they were to take such a step only by zeal for God's justice, and not by anger or revenge.[4] It should be remembered that the close of the twelfth century and the opening of the thirteenth were a period of enthusiasm for the monastic life and within which the influence of such a man as Bernard of Clairvaux was still strong, and when many both within and without the rapidly forming Orders were striving to live close to the letter of Christ's command.

In the time of Francis there were two peculiarly dramatic religious movements, with both of which every one is more or less familiar.

Those who have read Edward Everett Hale's *In His Name* have at least a romantic acquaintance with the noble company to whom neither Innocent nor his predecessors would give official recognition, and who were, in consequence, forced to exercise their freedom outside the Church. Peter Waldo had gone to the Pope; he had told him that he wanted literally to follow the command of Christ to sell all and become his disciple; he had said

[3]*Ibid.*, 292. [4]*Ibid.*, 294.

that he and his friends would preach and that they would read the word of God to those who might not in any other way have an opportunity to hear the Gospel. But Innocent and the contemporary Popes were suspicious of their zeal; they dreaded the multiplication of Orders; they refused to run the risk of sanctioning another over-enthusiastic society. The refusal was possibly the great mistake of the Popes of that time. Waldo persisted. The Waldensian Church was founded. In spite of all the vagaries of faith and conduct practised by many of the Waldenses, personal religion was intensified and enriched in Piedmont and in the Upper Rhone Valley. The poor had the Gospel preached to them. Their hunger for the direct word of God was so keen that they caused parts of the New Testament to be translated into their native tongue. Many of all classes had the Bible read to them. The spiritual revival was deep and sincere. But it remained without the official sanction of the Church.

The second movement was quite as sincere, and, with the higher-minded, quite as productive of good morals and vivid religion, but of an altogether different character. The Albigenses, who, for the most part, lived in southern France, were people of exceptional standards of thought and conduct. For people of their day their moral standards were high. Their religion was so vital and it played so practical a part in their daily lives that tens of thousands could not resist its contagious appeal. And yet Innocent and his immediate successors encouraged a crusade against them, and, stranger still, Simon de Montfort, whose kinsman was an English statesman of democratic tendencies, was among those who carried the crusade into ruthless effect. However, even those who are not in sympathy with Rome may understand the attitude of the Pope and of Western Europe toward these enthusiasts, for their social and religious points of view were incomprehensible to the average mind of their time and to many of able mind. They were vegetarians; they did not believe in marriage; they worshipped two gods, one of light, the other of darkness; they rejected the Old Testament, thinking it the product of the god of darkness. They formed a church organization closely parallel to the Roman form, but wholly independent of Papal direction or control. The worst of them, like the worst within the Church, were living perversely. It is, therefore, quite easy to see that the Albigenses would be looked upon as the enemies not only of the Church but of the State as well. People of their day could not imagine the survival of either religion or society if these high-minded but singular men and women were allowed to propagate their teachings. Nevertheless, and this is my reason for introducing them into this study of St. Francis, they greatly enriched the piety of the age; they increased the demand for vital religion; they emphasized the right of each man and woman to come into close contact with God. To them religion and life were of the same piece. Even though St. Dominic made it an ambition of his life to preach them back into the Church, and even though St. Francis would have looked askance at their virtues, they were among the factors that made the society of Francis's generation sensitive to the things of the spirit.

Such was the world into which Francis was born. Such was the world to the spiritual life of which he made his contribution.

It is not easy to say what kind of man St. Francis was physically, for descriptions differ radically. Thomas of Celano says that he was of moderate height, inclining to shortness[5] but otherwise a commanding personality. Thomas of Spoleto says, "His clothing was squalid, his bodily presence contemptible, his countenance unlovely." Chapter XIII of the Fioretti reads, "St. Francis was mean to look upon and small of stature." Sabatier, who evidently gathered his impression not so much from any one statement as from many descriptions, both indirect and direct, says, that Francis was less than middle height, that he had a delicate and kindly face, black eyes, a soft and sonorous

[5]Thomas of Celano, *The Lives of St. Francis of Assisi*. p. 81.

voice. There was in his whole person a delicacy and grace which made him infinitely lovely.[6] As in so many cases, it is quite evident here that descriptions do not altogether describe. Sabatier has chosen the better way of gathering his own impression from the description plus the effect the man had on those who came in contact with him. The saints were not all beautiful to look upon. Doubtless the stranger passed many of them by without so much as a glance in their direction. But to those who knew them there was a loveliness that could not be expressed in terms of physical charm. Both before his conversion and afterward men loved to be with Francis, and that one fact tells the whole story.

Peter Bernadone, the father of Francis, was a prosperous cloth merchant of Assisi. Having frequent occasion to go to France on business he became enthusiastically devoted to it; he admired its ways and its people; he cultivated its customs. It is not then to be wondered at that he changed the name of his son to Francis. In his father's absence the baby had been named John. But, as Mr. Chesterton has said, Peter would be content with nothing but Francesco, or "Frenchy."

From his earliest youth Francis was one of those open-hearted and big-hearted natures who are

[6]Paul Sabatier, *Life of St. Francis,* p. 182.

bound to be leaders either for good or for bad. A neighbor of foresight and insight might have said in those days that the boy would be a master of men, that neither the sinner nor the saint could resist him. From the very outset he was in for a good time and he had it. And from the beginning everybody's good time was the better if Francis was along. As he lived from day to day he showed that he had it in him to get more out of life than those with whom he worked and played. Whenever there was a merry party at Assisi Francis was to be found in the midst of the merrymakers; he was the arch-merrymaker. Within doors and out-of-doors his neighbors knew that he was the one who put the exhilaration into the daily occupation. Apparently, too, every one was glad to be somewhere near when the pranks were going on. The boy was contagiously masterful in his gaiety.

Some have said that his conduct in those days was not marked by moral self-restraint. Such a judgment is pure inference and nothing more. It is the consequence of that widespread feeling that one cannot have a really good time unless it is tinctured with evil. Frequently the suspicion is a consequence of the instinctive desire for contrast. The real saint must once have been a real sinner! Good Gregory the Great was a friend of the wicked Queen Brunhilda! John Bunyan played tip-cat in his unregenerate days! Florence Nightingale occasionally lost her temper! But this wish either to discover or to dwell upon sin in the life of one who has done the world good is unprofitable business. Whether Francis was a careless youth or a scrupulously careful one is not to the point. In either case he was a saint when not far from boyhood. And even in those formative years he showed many of the qualities which were later to direct his conduct. In doing wrong he may possibly have used those qualities of heart and head which were later all to be lavished on the right. But M. Jörgensen says that the friends of Francis well knew that they might speak of nothing vulgar in his presence, and that when any one of them risked anything of the kind the face of Francis showed signs of the strongest disapproval. And M. Jörgensen adds that like all the pure in heart Francis always had profound respect for the mystery of creation.[7]

But whatever else he was in those early days he was big-hearted—he was friendly and generous. From time to time Peter Bernadone would leave the cloth shop in the care of his son knowing possibly that when Francis was behind the counter customers liked to buy. As in all good trade there was the charm of attractive personal relationship,

[7]Based on *The Legend of St. Francis* by the Three Companions, chap. I, sec. 3, Eng. trans. Temple Classics.

as well as the excitement of making a good bargain. One can almost see the winning youth in the shop, the whole side of which was open to the street, enticing people in by the mere desire to have a chat with him and by the amusement that always accompanies friendly trade. Evidently the business of those days was not done as it is to-day —quickly, somewhat grimly, and with an eye only to the bargain itself. It was a leisurely affair. There was plenty of time. Conversation bulked larger than coin. Francis was strong in these qualities of the successful merchant. Trade flourished in the shop. Peter saw in Francis a means of greatly increasing the family income.

Francis's mind, however, was from time to time governed by almost prodigal impulses. On one occasion he was in the midst of an interesting bargain when a beggar interrupted him with an appeal for alms. Roughly repulsed, the beggar went empty away. But immediately Francis's conscience smote him. He said to himself, "What would I not have done if this man had asked something of me in the name of a count or a baron? What ought I not to have done when he came to me in the name of God? I am no better than a clown." Disposing of his customer he ran after the beggar and poured into his hands all the change he had. Francis had a big heart. And Francis's father was beginning to think that the profit gained in trade might be squandered in charity.

Francis was also chivalrous in the military sense of the word and in its finer inner meaning. While he was still hardly more than a boy Assisi and Perugia declared war against each other. Francis buckled on his armor and went out with the soldiers of Assisi. His men were defeated and Francis was thrown into prison, where he stayed for a year. At the end of what must have seemed a long period he was sent back to Assisi on an exchange of prisoners. It would be gratifying to know the thoughts that were running through his mind during those months of confinement. It is said that he was light-hearted and full of plans for the future. But remember that he was always light-hearted when his thoughts ran deep! He may even have been thinking of plans that were not communicated to his friends. For after he returned to Assisi he fell sick and after recovering from his illness a change seemed to have come over him. Illness is usually looked upon as a period of sheer waste; we cannot work; we cannot play! Therefore the days and weeks, possibly the months and years of illness, are lost! But such was not the case with many of the saints and such is not the case with many of the saintly. Illness frequently gives an opportunity to think; it affords leisure for reflection; it occasionally makes it impossible for the patient to do anything except to show his simple character, and in this he may be more like God than in the more active moments of his daily routine. Again it would be gratifying to know what was passing through the mind of Francis. It seemed as if he could hardly cease from the absorbing occupations of his daily life without reflecting upon possibilities of which he himself alone was conscious, even upon a future which might be a surprise to himself.

For a second time war broke out and Francis prepared to take his part. He equipped himself with sumptuous armor and started forth. But seeing one of his fellow-soldiers less well equipped than himself, with prodigal generosity he gave his armor to his friend. For a second time he fell sick. He could go no farther. He returned to Assisi, much to the surprise and somewhat to the disappointment of his family. And for the second time illness gave him an opportunity to think.

When he had recovered he returned to his friends and took up the old life of gaiety. It seemed as if he were to go back to the way of living that he had enjoyed so much before the wars and before his illness. But it was to be for only a short time. After Francis and his friends had had a glorious frolic and after his friends had trooped out-of-doors to carry their fun-making into the city, Francis was not to be found. Some of them returned to search for him. They saw him standing in the middle of the street, clothed in the gay garments of the king of the revels, and lost in a reverie. They brought him to himself by their shouts of friendly, derisive laughter and by their good-natured taunts that he had fallen in love. Much to their surprise and bewilderment he answered, "Yes, I am going to be married, but to a lady purer and more lovely than you have ever seen." The rich young merchant, the master of the revels, had gone out of his social circle for his bride; he had fallen in love with his Lady Poverty; he had discovered, perhaps during his imprisonment, perhaps during his illnesses, perhaps only by letting his own generous and big-hearted nature assert itself, that he would be happy only after he had sold all he had and had given to the poor. The saintly life had begun.

Francis had yet to taste the joy of his decision. Like so many of those who have left their mark on the religious life of the West, he went on a journey to Rome. There he visited many of the churches and shrines and there he made a critical test of his purpose. He exchanged clothes with a beggar, and all day long he stood in front of a church asking alms. He found himself extraordinarily happy, happier than he had ever been before. He had touched the outer edge of that life in which he was to find perfect freedom—a life in which he was to call nothing his own and in which he would have only himself to give.

Outwardly, however, Francis still looked the rich young man. He lived in his father's house; he dressed sumptuously; his purse was full; he rode the most spirited of horses. And it was when he was well-clothed and well-mounted that he learned the joy of forgetting himself and of losing his life in that of another. As he rode along one of the highways of Assisi he saw the most abhorrent and loathsome of all sights—a leper walking toward him. At once he drew rein, turned his horse and started in the opposite direction. At once also, in shame, he turned, rode toward the leper, dismounted, gave the leper money, and, as if the leper were one of the priests of God, kissed his hand. Again Francis's soul was filled with joy unspeakable. He had found the service of perfect freedom. And neither then nor after many years of caring for these wretched people did he become a leper. Unknown to himself may he not have discovered that unselfishness, readiness to serve, loss of self in the welfare of another, carry an immunity of their own? Only those who have not feared disease; only the physician, the priest, the parent, who have died to themselves and have risen again in the life of another, have discovered the secret of Francis's immunity, and can therefore understand it.

Francis was now hungry for the life of the spirit. Wherever he might be he sought for opportunities to know more of Christ and God and to help his fellow-men in ways near at hand. He seldom passed a church without going in. As he listened to the reading of the New Testament and heard the words of the Mass he forgot himself; he was oblivious to the priest. It was as if with his own ears he heard Christ speaking directly to him and as if with his own eyes he saw Christ's sacrifice for him and for men. He went into the hills and into the woods, and there among the trees and the flowers and the birds he felt very near his Lord. If there were any poor he tried to give them a helping hand; if there were any outcasts he gave them a word of cheer, and, better still, a start on another way of living. He was feeling his way along. He knew that he had found happiness, but he did not know whither he was going.

His father, however, seemed very certain that Francis was going the way of the spendthrift and the madman. He lost no occasion to upbraid his son for wasting time and money. He threatened him with all kinds of punishment. After a singular breach of obedience Peter Bernadone shut Francis in a small room of his house. But the father's opposition could hardly stem the tide of the son's new life, and in despair Peter laid the case before the good bishop of Assisi. It was but natural that the father should expect support from the bishop. It was but natural also that the bishop should try to take a dispassionate view of the dangerous disagreement between father and son.

The bewildered father and his incomprehensible child appeared before the bishop. Peter Bernadone poured forth the story filled with disappointment and bitterness. Francis listened in silence until his father had finished giving him a reputation for disloyalty and prodigality. He then gave back to his father the money he had taken for the restoration of St. Damian's Church. And, as if to clear himself of any obligation, he said to the bishop, "My Lord, not only the money which belongs to him, but also the clothes I wear, which are his, will I give back." He stripped himself naked—all save a hair shirt which the bystanders with surprise saw that he had been wearing next his skin. Again he spoke, this time to the people gathered in the bishop's court, "Hear all of ye and understand: until now I have called Pietro Bernadone my father; but because I propose to serve the Lord I return him his money, concerning which he was troubled, and all the clothes I had of him: for now I wish to say: Our Father who art in heaven, and not father Pietro Bernadone." It was a high-spirited thing to do. It did not display the sensitive sympathy that Francis afterward showed to those who had failed to understand him even more thoroughly than his father had. Peter was proud; he had had great social and business hopes with Francis at the heart of all of them. He was a hard man; his ambition for Francis took the form of his own will rather than that of the welfare of his son. He was one of those men who measure filial disloyalty by the failure or the unwillingness of a son to carry out the paternal plan. Yes, Peter was heavily at fault, just as many a father to-day, placed in a similar position, might be at fault. And Francis lived up to the letter of the Gospel! He repudiated his father that he might give himself wholly to God. It was one of the inevitable, but none the less deeply Christian, tragedies, carrying with it the waste incident to progress in Christianity.

Francis was now an outcast. But he was free. With remarkable speed, now that the pressure of all allegiance was taken off, he seemed to be advancing into the fulness of his power. He had seemed to hear the voice of Christ asking him to sell all and follow; he had heard another voice bidding him restore the ruined churches of St. Damian and Portiuncula. He had shaken off his reputation for boisterous hospitality and he was despised by his old friends. He was beginning to achieve a reputation for quiet kindliness and charity; those in great need began to look to him—the poor, the sinners, the sorrowing, the lepers, even men of gentle blood whose spiritual imagination was touched by this strange example of self-denial and of readiness to suffer and to serve.

It was not long before Francis found himself the centre of a little group of men ready to do as he directed. Together they worked, together they prayed and together they went about doing good. They fulfilled the wish of Francis to rebuild the little churches of St. Damian and Portiuncula, carrying and laying many of the stones themselves. They went where people's need was greatest, taking special charge of the most neglected—the lepers. And they did it all happily and in a way that made all about them happy. There was plenty of gloom in the conventional religion of the day. There was none in that of Francis and his friends. Such were the earliest Franciscans—the Franciscans before they had any rule.

The principles upon which these young enthusiasts lived were clear and simple.

They were to sell all they had, everything, and give to the poor. They were to take up the cross, that is, they were to suffer pain, pain of mind and pain of body, as they followed Christ. It was not a long constitution. But it was rather searching. These men lived up to it; they were not loose constructionists. In their zeal they frequently found themselves in positions that tested their sincerity, and invariably with a light heart and with a fine spirit they were true to their comforting ideal.

Seriousness and humor were mingled in working out the method of their lives. Francis had laid it down very clearly that he and his friends were not to be another social nuisance, another drain on society. Already there were enough of these. They were to pay their own way. Only as a last resort were they to accept a gift or to beg. For example—Brother Egidio started out for the Holy Land. Wherever the ship stopped in port he went ashore and turned his hand to the nearest work. Sometimes he would go about selling fresh water; again he made willow baskets; once he dug a grave.[8] If he could help it, no one should carry his weight. On one occasion a cardinal invited him to dinner. The hospitable prelate chuckled with pleasure at the thought that for once Egidio would be compelled to accept the gift of food. The cardinal's surprise, however, was great when he found that Egidio had gone into the kitchen, had swept it clean and had received from the cook some biscuits as wages, which he ate while the cardinal was proceeding through the various courses. Egidio overdid the rule, we might say. In his independence he made many kinds of hospitality impossible. And yet he may have been erring on the safe side; he may also have had a twinkle in

[8]Sabatier, *op. cit.*, p. 123.

his eye as he came back from the kitchen and took his seat by His Eminence.

There was also an easy and spontaneous generosity in the way they did their work, and a quick and sensitive reaction against any danger to benefit by their gains. The same Egidio had picked all the nuts from a very lofty walnut tree on condition that half should be his. He reaped a big harvest. His portion was so great an amount that he took it to Rome and made himself and many others happy by passing the nuts around to all the poor he met. On another occasion a woman had agreed with him on the price of a load of wood. When he delivered it she saw that he was a friar and therefore tried to overpay him. At once he said, "My good lady, I will not permit myself to be overcome by avarice." And he left her without taking a penny. Very foolish, yes! But very wise. It showed that he was master of himself.

Under all conditions, without exception, the brothers were to do as Christ would do. They were never to deviate in the slightest from this very straight and very narrow path.

> Now, in those times there were three famous robbers which did much evil in the country. They came to the hermitage one day to beg Brother Angelo to give them something to eat; but he replied to them with se-

vere reproaches, 'What! robbers, evil-doers, assassins, have you not only no shame for stealing the goods of others, but you would farther devour the alms of the servants of God, you who are not worthy to live, and who have respect neither for men nor for God your Creator. Depart, and let me never see you here again.' They went away full of rage. But behold, the saint returned, bringing a wallet of bread and a bottle of wine which had been given him, and the guardian told him how he had sent away the robbers; then St. Francis reproved him severely for showing himself so cruel. . . . 'I command thee by thine obedience,' he said, 'to take at once this loaf and this wine and go seek the robbers by hill and dell until you have found them, to offer them this as from me, and to kneel there before them and humbly ask their pardon and pray them in my name no longer to do wrong but to fear God; and if they do it, I promise to provide for all their wants, to see that they always have enough to eat and drink. After that you may humbly return hither!' Brother Angelo did all that had been commanded him, while St. Francis on his part prayed God to convert the robbers. They returned with the brother, and when St. Francis gave them the assurance of the pardon of God, they changed their lives and entered the Order, in which they lived and died most holily.[9]

Rather a fanciful way of dealing with bandits!

[9]Sabatier, *op. cit.*, p. 133. (Fior. 26.)

we say. Rather hazardous! Yes, but Jesus Christ would have dealt with them as Francis did. Without exception the Franciscans were to do as Christ would do. And because they did as Christ would do, and as Christ would do it, they were rewarded with Christ's results!

Paradoxical as it may seem, Francis and his friends were never so happy as when they were suffering. They believed in suffering; they sought it; they revelled in it; they triumphed in it. Not suffering for its own sake. Rather suffering that made them feel as if they were fellows with God and Christ to make the world better. Suffering was the sign of companionship. Francis and his friends had discovered, just as our Lord had discovered, that suffering was essential to progress. They were well aware that the time might come when there would be no more suffering. But they were quite as well aware that the time was very far off. They knew that suffering was an attribute, as it were, of Christ and of God. It was not by accident that the Testament of Francis fell open naturally at the story of the Passion, nor that his nearest friends discovered in his body the marks of the Lord.

One of the well-known stories will illustrate their conviction that suffering was joy and that joy was a sign of companionship with Christ. Francis was going with Brother Leo from Perugia to Santa Maria degli Angeli. It was a cold, wet day, and the wind was keen. Leo was walking a little ahead of Francis. Francis said, "O Brother Leo, may it please God that the Brothers Minor all over the world may give a great example of holiness and edification; write, however, and note with care that this is not the perfect joy." A few moments later he said, "O Brother Leo, if the Brothers Minor gave sight to the blind, healed the infirm, cast out demons, gave hearing to the deaf, or even, what is much more, raised the four days dead, write that not in this is the perfect joy." Again, "O Brother Leo, little sheep of God, if the Brother Minor could speak the language of angels, if he knew the courses of the stars and the virtues of plants, if all the treasures of the earth were revealed to him, and he knew the qualities of birds, fishes, and all animals, of men, trees, rocks, roots and waters, write that not in these is the perfect joy."

And with other statements of similar kind Francis challenged the curiosity of Brother Leo, until, almost impatiently, Leo answered, "Father, I pray you in God's name tell me in what consists the perfect joy." Francis was waiting for this question. He answered, "When we arrive at Santa Maria degli Angeli, soaked with rain, frozen with cold, covered with mud, dying of hunger, and we knock and the porter comes in a rage, saying,

'Who are you?' and we answer, 'We are two of your brethren,' and he says, 'You lie, you are two lewd fellows who go up and down corrupting the world and stealing the alms of the poor: Go away from here!' and he does not open to us, but leaves us outside shivering in the snow and rain, frozen, starved, till night; then, if thus maltreated and turned away, we patiently endure all without murmuring against him, if we think with humility and charity that this porter really knows us truly and that God makes him speak thus to us, then, O Brother Leo, write that this is the perfect joy. . . . Above all the graces and all the gifts which the Holy Spirit gives to his friends is the grace to conquer oneself, and willingly to suffer pain, outrages, disgrace and evil treatment, for the love of Christ.[10] Suffering and Joy! Suffering themselves into more perfect character! Suffering the world into likeness to the Kingdom of Heaven! Suffering themselves into complete unity with a suffering Christ and a suffering God, who through suffering are lifting the world and men up into perfection! Without suffering there is no consciousness of companionship with Christ and God! With suffering there is the serene assurance that men along with God are creating the new kingdom wherein dwelleth rightousness and peace!

Such were some of the qualities shown by Fran-

[10]Sabatier, *op. cit.,* p. 139. (Fior., 8.)

cis and the little group that were drawn to him. Although they bore the outward marks of extreme poverty—scantily clad, sometimes in rags, living in huts and hovels and caves and ruined churches—they were among the happiest of the happy. They had the mind of Christ and the people among whom they lived and whom they helped "took knowledge of them that they had been with Jesus."

But, after all, it was not the spirit and temperament of the first Franciscans so much as it was Francis himself that was so unusual and that drew men unto his way of life.

Unless one is willing to repudiate all wonder told of him (which I am not) he had an extraordinary power to heal. Not only men's minds and souls, but their bodies as well answered to his presence and his words. His power and his method with men seemed akin to that of Christ. Like the Apostles and their Master, the companions of Francis, as well as Francis himself, were almost daily with lepers. In fact, from the very outset of the movement it had seemed as if lepers were their special care. Had not a leper given Francis his first genuine joy in service?

On one occasion, however, it seemed as if there were a limit to philanthropy, a point beyond which the brothers could not go in their willingness to serve. They had tried to help a leper who had answered their unselfishness not only with insults, but with curses against the Virgin Mary and Christ. Apparently the brothers could put up with personal abuse, but not with blasphemy. In their despair, and yet unwilling to abandon the leper to his fate, they turned to Francis. Francis went to the leper. But Francis in turn was assailed with complaint and with abuse of those who had sought to help him. Francis at first tried to reason with the despairing man. He then prayed with him. Finding neither method of any avail he asked the leper what he would have him do. "Very well," the leper answered, "I wish you to wash me from head to foot, for I smell so bad that I disgust myself." At once Francis heated some water, making it fragrant with sweet-smelling herbs. He then took off the leper's clothes and began to bathe him from head to foot. And behold wherever the saint's hands touched the wretched body the flesh returned like the flesh of a little child. "And in proportion as the flesh was healed the soul of the wretched man was also healed." Such is the story. Yes, it seems a mere legend! A copy of the miracle-working of Jesus! Beyond belief! But before one casts away the story as incredible let him remember that few things are impossible to the completely unselfish, to those whose greatest happiness lies in service. Let him remember that there is no limit to the power of the man who lives wholly in the life of Christ. Let him remember that his share in the creative energy of God is in direct proportion to the quality of his unselfish affection. Francis had broken through the ordinary limits of human energy. He, through his utter self-forgetfulness, his love, had entered into the energies that are Christ's and God's, and yet, none the less, his own.

Unlike many, possibly most of the men of his day, Francis loved nature. And, unlike others of his time, there was no fear in his love. His outlook upon the world and upon everything within it was serene and trustful and friendly. As one surveys the past it is difficult to find another who shared the same feeling in the same way. One is rather reminded of a sentence in the Book of Genesis—And God saw all that He had made and behold it was very good. Francis had in some strange way discovered and mastered the divine point of view.

He loved the fields, the woods, the hills and the valleys. He was born in a city that nestles quietly on the slopes of Subasio. Daily as boy and young man he had but to lift up his eyes to sweep the Umbrian plain, the hills of northern Italy and the distant mountains. He had but to climb the summit of Subasio to see the Sibillini, the snow-capped peaks of the Apennines. As one runs through his life he seems to find an almost conscious selection of lovely, of beautiful, of grand regions within which to live. The Carceri is hidden in a gorge of Subasio, dark with the shade of trees, a brook which at times is a torrent, birds of many kinds—if one may assume that then it was much as it is now;[11] Lake Trasimeno, on an island in the middle of which he kept a forty-day fast, one of the beautiful lakes of Italy, with high hills rising from it to the north and west and with gently rolling country to the south; La Verna, the mountain on which he is said to have had his supreme union with Christ, well over three thousand feet high, the summit of which is flanked on the north with crags and precipices and covered with trees of magnificent girth and with wild flowers of many kinds. Francis seems to have shown his saintliness in his choice of homes.

It is said that on one occasion he passed through the city of Assisi and out through one of the city gates. The Umbrian plains and the distant hills lay before him. He stood still. He drew in a deep breath. He said not a word. He was speechless with the glory of it.

He seems to have had singular power over animals and birds. A few years ago I was sitting in my tent door at Squam Lake in New Hampshire reading Sabatier's *Life of St. Francis* and thinking in a leisurely way of what I was reading. As if

[11]The Carceri is now a *Zona di Refugio* for birds (no shooting allowed).

to make my thought clearer and to help me to understand St. Francis, one of the many kinds of warblers alighted in a bush not far from me. It searched among the leaves and branches utterly unafraid of me, but still at a safe distance. I doubt if it would have come nearer. I would not have harmed the bird. I should have been very happy if it had come to the branches about my tent. I should have been supremely satisfied if it had shown no fear and perfect trust. I had my illustration. Now I knew the difference between St. Francis and myself. I had no power to break down through the superficial parts of my nature and to give freedom to those deeper feelings which could have passed from me to the little bird and which would have drawn it to me in affection. I could not release my strong desires; I could not give freedom to my richer emotions; I could not be my true self. St. Francis had broken through the superficial crust of human nature. He could give his deepest longings, his richest affections, perfect expression. His love of a bird could pass out from him as an energy; it could draw the bird in confidence to his very feet. If I could but be myself I could have the power of Francis. Yes, like him, I could have the power of Christ. For it is all a matter of breaking through the crust of one's nature and releasing one's own natural powers.

Closely following my experience with the warbler I had another of a somewhat more fascinating type—again, as if to make clear to me what I was reading of St. Francis. As I sat at my tent door in the woods turning the pages of my book, I thought I saw out of the corner of my eye something moving in the underbrush. I looked around. Whatever it was, it stopped. I turned to my book, pretending to read. Again it moved, coming toward me. Again I looked. It stopped, now in a path about forty feet away. It was a pup fox. I longed to have the pretty little animal come nearer. But it stood stock still. Again I pretended to read. It slowly approached, stopped short when I turned to glance at it, began to walk slowly toward my tent, keeping close watch of me, and calmly, with hardly a trace of fear, walked by only about eight or ten feet away. I would not have harmed the little fox. I loved him. But I could not release my emotions with power. I could not turn them into an energy that would pass from me to him. I could not be myself. Here again I discovered the difference between Francis and myself. There was nothing superficial about Francis. All superficialities had been destroyed. He was fully himself. His affections, his loves were like those of Christ—great energies going out to create affection and love. The animals yielded to his power. He drew them all to himself. At last I could understand St. Francis. At last I could accept the truths that have given rise to the stories told of him by his friends and that are the motive of the fresco of Giotto.

There is something more than poetry in his expressions of affection for nature. The wind and the rain, the hail and the snow and the fire, were his little brothers and sisters—even when they gave him pain. They were part of the creation of God. Francis knew them as one of the family of God would know them. The birds and the beasts were his own kin—even the fiercest of them. Like his brothers and sisters they were spiritually close to him, for had they not, like himself, had their origin in God? As it were, like their elder brother, he saw them with the eyes of the great Father of the family. He dealt with them as such, and they recognized their kinship with him.

About two years before Francis died he had a deep longing to unite himself with Christ more fully. A good friend had given him La Verna, one of the mountains in a range lying to the east of the upper valley of the Arno. As I have said, its summit is quite perfect in its loveliness and grandeur—a region in which the spirit of Francis would find perfect freedom. Taking a few of his closest companions he journeyed toward the mountain and made ready for the ascent. He was already a sick man. His body was worn out. His spirit was for much of the time in another world. It was evident to his friends that he could not climb to the summit. So they persuaded him to ride a donkey. As they went slowly up the slopes the driver of the donkey turned to Francis and said, "Is it true that you are Brother Francis of Assisi?" When Francis said that he was, the peasant continued, "Very well, apply yourself to be as good as folk say you are, that they may not be deceived in their expectation; that is my advice." At once Francis got off the donkey, knelt before the peasant and thanked him for his counsel.

When the little company reached the cliffs near the summit, Francis withdrew apart by himself, asking his friends to protect him from all intrusion. He wanted to be alone with Christ and with God. Days and weeks he spent in coming into a divine companionship which he hoped would have neither end nor interruption. The suffering of Christ which was the thought that had filled his heart and mind and soul since he had first given himself to men now possessed his being with a vividness never before experienced.

> And since he did bear in his heart this fervor of love and continual remembrance of Christ's Passion, the Lord Himself being minded to manifest the same unto all the world, did adorn him in marvelous wise while yet living in the flesh with the special privilege of a singular distinction. For whilst in

> seraphic ardor of desire he was uplifted toward God, and was transfigured by the sweetness of partaking in His Passion into the likeness of Him who of His exceeding love was willing to be crucified—on a morning about the Feast of the Exaltation of the Holy Cross, whilst he was praying on the side of the mountain that is called Alverna, about two years before his death, there appeared unto him a Seraph having six wings, and between the wings having the form of a most beautiful man crucified, whose hands and feet were stretched out after the manner of a Cross, most evidently setting forth the image of the Lord Jesus. And with twain wings he veiled his head and with twain the rest of his body, and twain were spread forth to fly. When this vision disappeared, a wondrous flame of love abode in his heart, but on his flesh yet more wondrously appeared the mark of the Stigmata of our Lord Jesus Christ, the which the man of God in so far as he might concealed unto his death, not being minded to make public the sacred mystery of the Lord, natheless, he could not so entirely hide it but that it were known at least unto his most intimate companions.[12]

Such is the story told by "The Three Companions." Yes, it is utterly abnormal. One may with difficulty accept it. And if one should accept it he would be reckoned among the credulous, the superstitious. And yet there the story stands,

[12] *The Legend of St. Francis,* by The Three Companions. Temple Classics, pp. 106–107.

written down by contemporaries, friends of Francis, accepted as a fact from the beginning. So far as literary evidence is concerned, a more promptly attested fact than any incident in the life of Francis's Master! Whatever may be one's attitude toward the story, and particularly if he wants to judge it fairly, ought he not to appraise the story in the light of the character of Francis? For more than fifteen years Francis had given himself lavishly to the service of men; for more than fifteen years he had been increasingly happy in that service; for more than fifteen years he had gone about among the poor, the diseased, the lepers; for more than fifteen years he had with peculiar sympathy made their suffering his own; for more than fifteen years he had lived in the light of the discovery that only when he suffered with men could he help them; for more than fifteen years he had read of the Passion of Christ (his New Testament opened of itself at the story of the Crucifixion) and had found that only when he was suffering for the sake of Christ in work that Christ would approve was he fully conscious of God. That was the mind of Francis. For more than fifteen years he had lived the life of Christ, he had fed upon the words of Christ, he had thought the thoughts of Christ, he had had the mind of Christ. A man like that is fully himself; he has reached the measure of the stature of the fulness of Christ;

he has found his essential power; like Christ, like God, he has become a creator; nature begins to move at his desire. To be one with Christ for fifteen years (and fifteen years is a long time) is to share the experience of Christ, even to the death of the Cross.

Worn in body, dead, yet alive in soul, Francis went down the mountain and back to work. His mighty spirit was burning up his frail body. And is there a better way than this to die? To have one's body burned away by the spirit! He knew that he had not long to live. He prepared for the end. He met death singing, for he was serenely conscious that he was but passing from one of the many mansions of God to another. Welcome my sister, Death! He ordered bread to be brought. He blessed it and brake it and handed to each a morsel to eat.[13] He forgave all. He blessed his brethren. He blessed Assisi. He asked that he might be stripped of his clothing and laid upon the ground that he might die in the arms of his Lady Poverty, "a wife more beautiful, more rich, more pure than you could ever imagine."[14] "And one of the brothers, a holy man, at the same moment, saw a brilliant orb of light borne by a little cloud, ascending as it were across many waters in a straight course to heaven."[15]

[13]Thomas of Celano, *op. cit.*, p. 345.
[14]Sabatier, *op. cit.*, pp. 23, 341.
[15]Father Cuthbert, *Life of St. Francis of Assisi.*

## CHAPTER VI

### IGNATIUS LOYOLA

Even though the Jesuits have, at certain periods of their dramatic history, laid themselves open to hostile criticism, little of an adverse character has been said of the men who formed The Society of Jesus and nothing of the genius whose heart and mind were its cause and its life. From the moment Ignatius Loyola's purpose was perceived and understood the West has looked upon him, if not with sympathy and agreement, at least with respect. Recently, however, as toleration has become more prevalent and as the unprejudiced students of religious experience have grown in number, he has become an object of the profoundest study, and the quality of his spiritual life has had a very wide appeal.

To illustrate this growing and thorough interest in Ignatius it is necessary only to direct the attention to certain books that have appeared within the last few years, books that not only give the facts of his life, but that show the hold he has, even after these four hundred years have gone by, on those of serious religious purpose. Mr. Henry Dwight Sedgwick published his *Ignatius Loyola* in 1923. A few years previously Father

Longridge, of the Anglican Order of St. John the Evangelist, published his translation of *The Spiritual Exercises,* together with the first translation into English of the *Directory.*[1] Father Longridge prepared his edition of *The Spiritual Exercises* to stimulate the interest and meet the needs of Anglicans who either themselves want to strengthen their own spiritual life after the manner of Ignatius, or who wish to follow Ignatius in conducting a retreat.[2] Romanists also have made excellent studies of Ignatius and the Order of Jesuits. It is remarkable, however, that much of the recent literature is from the hands and apparently from the hearts of non-Romanists.

The reason for not only the printing of these books, but also for the avidity with which they are being read, is that Ignatius is a religious marvel, and that he makes an appeal to the earnest Romanist and non-Romanist. To-day we are catching a little of John Wesley's enthusiasm for the man who at once, like St. Francis, supported the tottering walls of Rome and had a message for every seeker after God. The pathos of his young manhood, the romance of his turn to religion, his appeal to young men, the vividness of his spiritual experience and the dramatic success of the Society's early days, are not only matters

[1]*The Spiritual Exercises of Ignatius Loyola, with Commentary and Directory,* by W. H. Longridge.

[2]In 1926 Prof. Paul van Dyke's *Ignatius Loyola* appeared.

fascinating to the reader, but material upon which to base a more vital personal and corporate religious life. We turn with eager interest to the life of one who knew God and who made Him real to his companions.

Ignatius was born in the Spanish castle of Loyola near the village of Azpeitia, not far from the Bay of Biscay and close to the French border. For centuries that part of Spain had been a refuge and a stronghold for the faithful Catholics while the more central portions of the country were dominated by the Moors. It was a nursery of vigorous and militant Romanism.

Ignatius came into the world in 1491, the year before Columbus discovered America.[3] In other words, he was born at a moment when the minds of men were aflame with enthusiasm for adventure. Although hardly anything is known of his boyhood and youth, there is a story that while still very young he was adopted by an uncle and that he served as a page at the court of King Ferdinand. Whether or not there be any foundation for the report, it may be taken as a symbol of his contact with a world in which so much of dramatic interest was taking place.

Not only were these the days in which Spain and Portugal were absorbed in voyages of discovery, but the life of Ignatius spanned a period

[3]Mr. Sedgwick prefers 1495.

during which the modern world came into being. They were the days in which the contemporaries of Ignatius were exerting an influence in their respective fields as far-reaching as that of Ignatius was destined to be in religion. While Ignatius was an infant Lorenzo de Medici was gathering about himself painters, architects, sculptors and men of letters—men of enterprise, enthusiasm and genius. Raphael was born in 1487; he died in 1520 while Ignatius was laying out his plan of life. Copernicus finished his work in 1543 shortly after Ignatius had asked the Pope to recognize the Order of Jesuits and had begun his work in Rome. Galileo was born only eight years after Ignatius died. To mention such names is sufficient to show that Ignatius lived at a time when the imagination was sensitive and productive. That he should dream of a richer spiritual world, and that he should abandon his life to the joy of its realization, was simply one aspect of the era of discovery and accomplishment.

Parallel movements were also a manifestation of the vigorous moral, religious and ecclesiastical ambitions of his day. Ignatius was twenty-six years old when Martin Luther nailed his theses on the Wittenberg church door, and thereby not only inflicted a heavy wound on Rome, but stimulated the beginning of many of the independent national Churches of the North. Ignatius was a witness of nearly all the dramatic movements of the Reformation, for he was but seven years younger than Luther and he outlived him by eleven years. He was eighteen years older than Calvin, but Calvin had made an earlier start in his campaign to consecrate his own will and the wills of the people to the will of God. Ignatius was hardly out of the University in Paris when in the kingdom of France the interest in Luther changed to an interest in Calvin.

As a background to the life and work of Ignatius the separation from Rome of some of the nations must not be forgotten. Later attempts on the part of the Jesuits to win back to Rome both Sweden and England remind one vividly that these nations left the Roman allegiance not only after Ignatius had reached years of maturity, but after he had begun to ask himself how he could best help the Church. He was at the University of Alcalá, training his mind for his work, when Gustavus Vasa threw in his lot and that of Sweden with the Reformation. He was at the University of Paris securing the mental discipline, without which he knew he could not rightly serve God, when England determined to revert to an earlier and purer type of Catholicism and therefore repudiated the Roman supremacy. To confine ourselves only to England, it throws light on the later solicitude of Ignatius for the nations to remember that when he was forty years old England was still within the Roman Communion and that when he died in 1556 England had tried the non-Papal Romanism of Henry VIII, the moderate and the radical Anglicanism under Edward VI and Cranmer, and had, under Mary Tudor and her husband, Philip II, Ignatius's own king, returned temporarily to the Roman fold.

The generation of Ignatius, therefore, spans one of the most dramatic periods in human experience. Men were discovering new worlds in practically every department of thought and action. While the Mediæval World was by no means being forgotten, the modern world was coming into being.

It would be wrong, however, to suppose that all the religious and moral contribution of the first half of the sixteenth century was being made by the non-Roman Churches and that Rome itself was in a state of hopeless decadence. Before Ignatius died the Counter Reformation had set in. It is an error in historical judgment to look upon it as merely a form of retaliation against Protestantism. It was quite as honest an attempt on the part of Rome to purify itself in head and members as the reforming Churches of the North were sincere in their struggle for simpler forms of worship, and for a religion in closer harmony with the New Testament and sober tradition.

The three great agencies of Roman reform were the Council of Trent, the Inquisition and Index, and the Order of Jesuits. Trent, largely guided in theology and morals by the Jesuits, was the last of many earnest attempts so to state the Faith that it would commend itself to men of intelligence, and so to cleanse the conduct of the Church that saints might be satisfied with it. The council in large measure met these needs. Men like Carlo Borromeo and St. François de Sales were not likely to remain within a Church whose faith was folly and whose morals were rotten. The Inquisition and the Index, terrible engines for the suppression of individual opinion and of pioneering thought, must be examined in the light of their time. Only those who think that force ought never to have been applied to religion, and only those who think that reading should be altogether uncensored, will fail to distinguish between Rome's attempt and the form of its attempt. In those days to wander from the well-marked path was thought to be insanity. The wanderer was dealt with as a maniac. To appeal to his reason was insanity in only another form. Just to chasten our judgment let us remember that England was practising the inquisitional method at the same time, although its persuasions were imprisonment and the block rather than hot pincers and the rack.

Let us also remember that there is a strong

demand to-day for the suppression of kinds of books no more dangerous to us than heretical books seemed to them. If Philip II was a royal saint (and some claim that he was) his suppressive measures were well intended. The tragedy of it was that he was one of the last to whom such measures seemed either necessary or right. The Counter Reformation had a high-minded purpose. Without doubt there were ignorant, evil-minded and cruel men in power at the time, as there always are in moments of transition whether in Church or State. But the men who were largely responsible for the direction of thought and conduct were men of consecration. They were meeting the needs of those to whom the Protestant Reformation meant spiritual bankruptcy. Although they were mediævally minded (and this is not necessarily an insult) they were agents of the spirit to countless men and women of their day. Ignatius, in person, and through those of his spiritual fellowship, brought intelligence and moral vigor to the Church of Rome.

It is sometimes said that a man speaks for his native land, that he reflects the ideals of his country. If such was the case with Ignatius, one must think that the Spain of his day was ready to live and die for the Church and God. Sometimes a man will die for his friends; very seldom, if ever, has a nation consciously died for another nation.

We like to think that Belgium was ready to do so; the evidence is sufficient to prove that she was. Mr. Sedgwick has quoted from the Spanish historian Menendez y Pelayo to show that the Spain of Ignatius's day loved religion more than territory.

> Let politicians and political economists laugh their fill, but if we are to choose between the maritime greatness of England under her Virgin Queen, and the slow martyrdom and impoverishment of our nation, which during two centuries was the unselfish arm of the Church, every heart that beats with enthusiasm for the noble and the beautiful, will not hesitate to bestow the palm on us. I grant that in all these epic feats of knightly prowess there was some mixture of blind, narrow, national pride; but that too had a noble origin, for we did not look upon ourselves as a nation born to command and other nations destined to obey, but we ascribed our feats to God as their source and origin, narrowing all our vain glory to the belief that God, in reward of our faith, had chosen us, as once He chose the people of Israel, to be His sword in battle, the instrument of His justice and His vengeance upon apostates and sacrilegious men; and therefore every man among our soldiers, from the mere fact that he was a Catholic and a Spaniard, believed himself a Judas Maccabæus.[4]

[4]H. D. Sedgwick, *Ignatius Loyola,* p. 30. By permission of The Macmillan Company, publishers.

It is reasonable to think that Ignatius was of such a mind.

When Ignatius was thirty years old, in 1521, he was defending the border fortress of Pampeluna against the French. He was already a soldier of ability and knightly character. But for him and an officer of similar courage the Spaniards would have abandoned the fortress. Before the final assault Ignatius confessed to a soldier companion and in turn the soldier confessed to him. "After the walls were destroyed, Ignatius stood fighting bravely until a cannon ball broke one of his legs and injured the other."[5] His French captors were chivalrous. They showed him the favor that a man of distinguished character would naturally receive. The broken leg was set. They gave him the best of care and bore him on a litter to his father's castle. But when it was found that the leg had been badly set Ignatius submitted to another operation. The leg was again broken and reset. "He uttered no word and gave no sign of suffering save that of tightly clenching his fists."[6] His physical troubles, however, were not yet over. Ignatius was a handsome man and he knew it. He liked to appear well before the world. After the second setting a bone protruded below the knee. This must be remedied if he was ever to

[5 and 6] *Autobiography*, edited by Ed. O'Conor, p. 20.

appear at Court without embarrassment. Again, with fortitude that excited his elder brother's wonder and admiration, he endured the pain.

Although Ignatius came through his troubles with sound health he had gone down close to death's door. He had even prepared for death and had taken the last Sacrament. The weeks of suffering, the familiar thought of death, and the leisure that illness always brings to review one's life, set his mind running very deeply. Being also an active-minded man he was not content with dreaming away the days. At the castle they could not give him the fiction he wanted. But they gave him all they had—*The Life of Christ* by Ludolph and the *Flowers of the Saints*.[7] His thoughts, his reading and his desire to make his life count for some kind of good, soon determined his future. If he could not be a soldier of his King he would be a soldier of Christ. He would emulate the saints. He willed to be a saint and he became one.

We all admire the saints, but we do not quite like to have a saint living under the same roof. We would rather have him live next door or in the next town or in some foreign land, or in some other country—far enough away to relieve us of too great moral and religious pressure. Ignatius was aware that his brother would not sympathize

[7]A book of stories of the saints.

with his new purpose. So with pardonable guile he determined to slip away under another pretext and to begin his new life as he would. Clad as a knight he started in the direction of Navarre, discharged some business there (just to ease his conscience) and then turned with significant determination toward the shrine of Montserrat. He had read that knights would pass the dark hours until morning in vigil at the altar of the Virgin; he would do so too. On his way to Montserrat he fell in with a Saracen. Being a friendly man, doubtless even such an heretical companionship was welcome to him. But, being bent upon a mission, the conversation was likely to take a religious turn. The Saracen was not willing to grant to Mary the unique nature which the Church claimed for her. Ignatius was shocked and angered. As the Moslem drew away into the distance Ignatius did not know whether to hurry after the Mohammedan and slay him for his blasphemy or to allow him to go in peace. Characteristically, he left the decision with God, which, in this case, meant that he left it to the chance direction his horse might take. When he came to a fork in the road the horse threw in his vote for peace by taking the way toward the shrine. The Saracen and the horse were probably unaware that they had helped to found the Order of Jesuits.

Ignatius had made for himself a garment of the

coarsest sackcloth, had given away his knightly apparel, had hung up his armor before the shrine and had passed the night in vigil. The saintly life had begun.

The next day he journeyed on to the neighboring monastery at Manresa where he stayed for about a year. When he went away he had practised, and probably largely written, his *Spiritual Exercises,* and he had brought his body and mind and spirit to a point of perfection which was to last throughout his life. Apparently while he was at Montserrat he had been shown a book of Spiritual Exercises written by Francisco Garcia de Cisneros. Evidently it had taken strong hold on him as a method for mastering one's self and becoming more vividly aware of God, but undoubtedly it became the general basis for his own method of moral and religious development. There can be little question that his own *Spiritual Exercises* are intensely autobiographic. He had lived the system and it had worked. In fact he was so convinced that it would do for others what it had done for him that he went through it with each one of those whom he would help religiously. It may not be an exaggeration to say that from the beginning every one connected with the Order has followed the method of Ignatius.

The method is simple, concrete and very exacting. A director supervises the participant for "four weeks," the "weeks" being shorter or longer than seven days according to the needs of the one undergoing the discipline. The purpose of the *Exercises* is to make all the truths of religion as real as the facts of daily life. To achieve this end an increasingly powerful concentration of the attention is practised.

The first week is given to thoughts of creation, sin and death, the second to the daily life of Jesus, the third to the passion and redemptive work of Christ, the fourth to His heavenly activity. To every detail of each the individual brings his whole being, his thought in the forms of imagination and contemplation. A few sentences from the *Exercises* will suggest the process and its probable effect.

> Thou hast taken me from the abyss of nothing . . . present yourself before God like a criminal who appears at the tribunal of justice. . . . Taste in spirit all the bitterness, the tears, the regrets, the remorse of the damned. . . . Listen to the monotonous sound of the clock which measures your last hours. . . . Reflect upon the obedience of the boy and the child Christ. . . . Be with Jesus while He prays, while He works. . . . Watch the way He deals with Zacchæus, the Samaritan, the Magdalen. . . . Contemplate our Saviour present in the tabernacle and impatient to give Himself to you. . . . Respire the celestial perfume of the divinity and the

> humanity of Jesus Christ. . . . Place your finger in His wounds and convince yourself of His love. . . . Represent to yourself Christ rising gloriously from the tomb. . . . Ask yourself . . . What have I done hitherto for heaven? What ought I to do for heaven? What shall I do henceforth for heaven?[8]

Such are some of the characteristic passages taken almost at random from *The Spiritual Exercises.* Allowing for the beliefs about hell and heaven current in the sixteenth century it would be difficult to conceive of a discipline more effective for making real the primary truths of the spiritual life. At all events we know that "four weeks" of concentration on such subjects as these brought to Ignatius and his friends not only certitude but enthusiasm.

After passing through the content of the *Exercises* himself he no longer had any doubts as to the humanity and the divinity of Christ, nor as to the mystery of Christ's presence in the Sacrament, nor as to the mystery of the Trinity.

> Often in prayer, and even during a long space of time did he see the humanity of Christ with the eyes of the soul. At the elevation of the body of Christ our Lord he beheld, with the eyes of his soul, white rays descending from above. Although he cannot after so long an interval explain the

[8]*Autobiography,* p. 56.

> details of this vision, still the manner in which our Lord Jesus Christ is present in the Blessed Sacrament was clearly and vividly stamped upon his mind.[9]
>
> Once while reciting on the steps of the monastery the 'Little Hours' in honor of the Blessed Virgin, his vision carried him beyond the earth. He seemed to behold the Blessed Trinity in the form of a lyre or harp; this vision affected him so much that he could not refrain from tears and sighs. . . . Such an impression was made on him on that occasion that during his after life he experienced great devotion.[10]

Furthermore, the discipline to which he had subjected himself had produced an effect quite contrary to that common to the ordinary man. Whenever his mind was undistracted by conversation, by business, or by any of the throng of interests that clamored for his attention, it turned at once, without the slightest effort of attention, to awareness of companionship with Christ and God. With most men awareness of the presence of God is rare; absorption in passing events and duties is common. By an act of will we turn from the world to God. With Ignatius the daily routine was an interruption, albeit a necessary interruption, in a life of vivid feeling that God was by his side. God-consciousness was his normal mood.

[9] *Autobiography*, p. 56. [10] *Ibid.*, pp. 53, 54.

Some of us are tempted to say that *The Spiritual Exercises* are overwrought and that Ignatius emerged from his weeks of spiritual discipline an unbalanced enthusiast, if not a fanatic. Such a judgment is common. In fact, until very recent days it has been generally held by Protestants. But a judgment of this kind disposes of no problems: it leaves Ignatius totally unexplained. We know that Ignatius was a spiritual giant; we know that the discipline represented by *The Spiritual Exercises* made him such. Is it then far from the truth to say that *The Spiritual Exercises* were not merely a self-devised method by which a man has blundered into a certain type of spiritual experience, but rather a method created by that strange union of the Divine Mind and the human through which temperaments of a certain type become aware of the reality of religious truth? And may it not be right to say that whatever the form of the experience at which the discipline arrives, beyond the borders of ordinary experience though it may be, the words "imagination" and "hallucination" do not dispose of it? Rather may it not be permissible to say that the form itself may be the language chosen by God himself, by means of which He speaks to a certain type of mind? I hardly see how one can come to any other conclusion without ignoring the experience of one who brought God and Christ and the institutions of the Church permanently, vividly and usefully to himself and to countless others, or without thinking that God is frightfully wasteful in His processes of revelation.

We are confronted with the problem of rightly appraising a system and an experience which lie at the centre of the Jesuits' spiritual life, an experience, in its first generation, of a remarkably unique kind. When Ignatius tells us that he lays claim to no greater religious experience than that of the Saints, but that he "would not exchange experience with the Saints" we are involved in the dilemma of either rejecting the experience or of taking seriously the method by which he attained to it and the detail of the experience itself. It is conceivable that God deals with the individual in ways most sensitively adapted to the needs of the individual—possibly in ways which only He and those of like spiritual nature can understand, ways also which may be utterly unsuited to another type of mind and therefore incomprehensible to it.

However, assured of the reality of his experience and eager to pass it on, not only to some one else, but to those who to his mind were of strategic importance to the success of the universal Church, he made his way to the Holy Land. Like St. Francis, three centuries before him, he wanted of course to stimulate his own devotional life by a visit to the holy places, but also to meet the infidel in the land so closely associated with the life of his Master. Utterly without means, assisted by charity and the kindness of the ship's captain, he reached his destination. His stay was short. He was probably too uncompromising to be a guarantee of peace between Moslem and Christian. He was probably sufficiently impolitic and untactful to try to convert the least convertible—to turn the Moslem to Christ. As Mr. Sedgwick suggests, "he hoped to convert the Turks and win Jerusalem single-handed."[11] Whatever the facts were, the Prior of the Franciscan monastery refused to allow him to stay. Dutifully, Ignatius took ship and returned to the West.

Thus far his experience had proved to him that he had firm hold on the truths of religion, but experience had also proved that he would be an ineffective worker for the Church until his mind could be a better servant of his spirit. Consequently he determined to go to school. At thirty-three years of age he put himself under a master and began the study of Latin. At thirty-five he began the study of philosophy at the University of Alcalá. He was fully and frankly aware that his general information was scanty and that the rudiments of the information he already possessed were insufficient. In order to lay firm foundations

[11]*Op. cit.*, p. 44.

he was not ashamed to sit on the same bench with children. From Alcalá he went to Salamanca and from Salamanca to Paris, spending practically ten years at the universities and issuing from the last with a mind that would not hinder the expression of his soul.

But let it not be thought that his religious work was allowed either to cease or to pause. Wherever he happened to be he gave *The Spiritual Exercises* to those whom he wanted to help. At Alcalá and at Salamanca he and his companions were suspected and imprisoned because of their zeal and peculiar method of dress. In Paris he gathered about himself the small group of men who, later, were to be the first members of the Society of Jesus. Although during these years his primary duty was study, and although he was repeatedly enjoined by the Inquisition and the universities not to trespass on the domain of religious instruction, yet the work went on and the spiritual friendships grew in number. These were the years in which he was joined by Pierre Lefévre, Francis Xavier, Diego Lainez, Alfonso Salmerón, Simon Roderiguez and others—many of whom were to become eminent as men of religion, as teachers, theologians, missionaries and saints.

Although Ignatius and his friends were bound together in the strongest spiritual sympathy it was not until much later that they asked Papal permission to found a new order. While they were in Paris they were content to work quietly and to develop their own devotional life. They were also preparing for a mission to the Holy Land, or, in case this were to prove impracticable, for any work the Church might give them to do. More as individual servants of the Church than as a society they took the vows of poverty and chastity in St. Mary's on Montmartre. In other words they were a group of spiritually congenial friends, drawn together by the genius of Ignatius, and, because of his unselfish and masterful leadership, eager to do anything for God. Ignatius was their rule. His will remained their rule until he died some twenty years later.

At this point, however, the Society of Jesus begins to emerge, for their resolve to go to the Holy Land was soon changed to a determination to remain in Italy and place themselves at the disposal of the Pope.

Years of extreme asceticism had so weakened the health of Ignatius that he yielded to persuasion to rest and recuperate in Spain. Before he went, however, he planned with his friends that they were to gather in Venice in about a year and then decide upon their policy for the future. At the appointed time they met. Picture the group. Every one a man of vivid religious experience; every one a man of thorough training and of unusual intellectual ability; every one ready for service. Wholly dependent upon charity, living in ruined churches and abandoned buildings, daily helping the outcasts and encouraging the fallen, they slowly made their way from Venice to Rome, Ignatius being intentionally the last to arrive there. Ignatius feared that they would meet with opposition, for he thought that he had an enemy in Caraffa, later Paul IV, and in Dr. Ortiz, Charles V's ambassador; but the former proved a cautious friend and the latter asked Ignatius to direct him through *The Spiritual Exercises.* Throughout these months Ignatius was conscious of the peculiar companionship and comfort of Christ. "One day, when he was a few miles from Rome, he entered a church to pray, and there felt his soul so moved and changed, and saw so clearly that God the Father placed him with Christ His Son, that he did not dare to doubt it."[12]

While Ignatius and his friends were waiting in Rome for official recognition they did the work the Pope gave them to do. With the enthusiasm and vivid religion of Ignatius as their inspiration they became teachers of theology and workers among boys, orphans and fallen women. Again, during these weeks and months Ignatius was in a state of spiritual exaltation. And yet it would be difficult to imagine a man in calmer possession of

[12]*Autobiography,* p. 140.

all his faculties. He might, in a vision, see his friend Hozes entering heaven; he might also be giving most practical thought to the organization of the Society.

The processes by which he determined upon the final form of the Constitution and his attitude toward his own election as general of the Order bear the marks of that singular union of the spiritual and the practical which were peculiar to him throughout his life. In fact they would seem to prove that the essentially practical must always be spiritual. "He told Father Gonzales de Camara that, while he was at work on the Constitution, he used to say Mass every day and to lay each several article before the Lord and pray over it."[13] When he turned his attention to the election of a general it was at once evident that he himself, very much against his will, would be chosen. For three days the Fathers prayed for heavenly direction. The ballots were cast. All the ballots, save his own, were for Ignatius. At once he refused to serve, saying that he had not himself sufficiently in subjection, and how then could he direct others? Mr. Sedgwick has rightly asked the reader to believe in the genuineness of such humility.[14] The brethren yielded to his demand for another election. They cast their ballots again with a similar result. What was Ignatius to do? He left the de-

[13]See Sedgwick, *op. cit.*, p. 215. [14]*Ibid.*, p. 214.

cision to God and his confessor. He went into seclusion in San Pietro in Montorio, confessed every sin from his youth up that he could recall (and there were plenty to confess), and then his spiritual adviser told him that to refuse would be contrary to the will of the Holy Spirit. He accepted as whole-heartedly as he had refused.

The members of the Order quickly scattered over Europe, while Ignatius remained in Rome. They became the most skilful teachers of youth; they went on distant and dangerous missions; they were in demand as theologians of the Church. Wherever they could say the word that would support Romanism they said it with persuasive power. Their lives and their ability commended their point of view to the high-minded and the thoughtful.

As long as Ignatius lived he followed them with affectionate and sensible counsel. When, for example, at the Pope's request, Ignatius asked Lefévre, Lainez and Salmerón to put their faith and their training at the disposal of the Council of Trent he gave them very homely advice. He said if he himself were to go he would speak slowly, after reflection, and in a friendly spirit; he would listen quietly in order to understand the kind of mind the speakers might have; he would enumerate the reasons on both sides; he would give an opinion with the utmost calmness and mod-

*From "The Life of St. Ignatius and the Early Jesuits" by Stewart Rose. Catholic Society Publishing Co.*

PAPAL CASTLE OF TIVOLI, WHERE PAUL III APPROVED THE CONSTITUTION OF ST. IGNATIUS

esty; he would suit the convenience of the other person, in order to arouse him to the greater glory of God.[15] It was good advice, and, on the whole, well followed. The conduct of his men was manly and Christian.

Possibly, however, the kind of man he was from day to day in the routine of life will reveal his character as fully as it was shown in any of the more dramatic episodes. He began the day with an hour of meditation. After attending Mass he turned to business, never making an important decision without prayer and reference to those whose counsel might be of value. His conversation after dinner was on subjects of spiritual character; it was followed by correspondence. In the evening he prepared for the work of the next day, "talked with his secretary, walked up and down the room with a stick, for with age his wounded leg limped a little, and closed the day by a complete surrender to Holy thoughts." Many hours must have been spent in prayer, for he allowed himself only four hours for sleep. He loved music, but he indulged in it only when he was not well, thinking it a luxury.[16] He was patient, very fair, severe, but only when severity was an expression of unselfishness. His self-control was complete—"If this misfortune were to fall on me, provided it

[15]See Sedgwick, *op. cit.*, pp. 256, 257.
[16]*Ibid.*, p. 330.

happened without any fault of mine, even if the Society were to melt away like salt in water, I believe that a quarter of an hour's recollection in God would be sufficient to console me and to reestablish peace within me."[17]

His self-surrender was complete—"He asked Lainez what would he do if God were to give him the choice between immediate death and everlasting glory and continued life with a final reward depending on the quality of his effort, knowing that with a longer life he might render God greater service. Lainez answered that for his part he would choose at once to enter into the joy of his Lord and make sure of his salvation. 'By heavens, not I,' Ignatius said. 'If I could do the meanest service to God I would beseech Him to leave me here until that task were done; I should look to His interest more than to mine.' "[18]

He died as he had lived, calmly and with preparation. He asked for the blessing of the Pope. Seriously ill though he was, the evening before he died he supped with his physician and Master Polanco. An hour after sunrise he passed away into another of the many mansions of God—into a world as real to him as this. A man who in the turbulent days of transition from mediæval to modern times was strangely intimate with God,

[17]*Encyclopædia Britannica,* see Loyola.
[18]See Sedgwick, *op. cit.,* p. 352.

and one who brought sublime religious assurance to the lives of many! A noble character to whom God spoke in a language he could understand and to which his whole soul made intelligent response! A challenge to us all to widen and deepen our religious sympathies and not to imagine that our own religious experience is the total truth!

# CHAPTER VII

## PIUS IX

Two dramatic events fell within the pontificate of Pope Pius IX. The first was the declaration of Papal Infallibility by the Vatican Council on July 18, 1870. The second was the entrance into Rome of the Italian army on September 20, 1870, and the seizure of Rome for the capital of the new United Kingdom of Italy. Within nine weeks, therefore, the Papacy was carried to its highest point of spiritual authority and driven to its lowest point of temporal authority. After the Vatican Council the Pope's utterances were to be considered without error whenever he spoke officially on matters of morals and faith. And after September 20 the Papal possessions included hardly any more than the properties of the Vatican and the Lateran. It seemed almost as if the prophecy of Joachim of Floris were coming true. In about the year 1200 he said that if the Church would only withdraw from the world it would become spiritually supreme. Since 1870 the Papal income has not been allowed to suffer; and the faithful have been loyal to Rome as seldom before.

Giovanni Maria Mastai Ferretti was born in 1792. He died in 1878. He was elected Pope in

1846. His pontificate is the longest in Papal history, having exceeded "the years of Peter"[1] by seven. He was born at Sinigaglia of parents whose traditions of nobility ran back three or four centuries. He received the usual education of a boy of his social position. When he came to the point of deciding how he should spend his life he set his heart on entering the Papal Guard. Cardinal Consalvi, Pope Pius VII's Secretary of State, one of the ablest and noblest of Papal statesmen, resolutely and finally refused to receive the young Mastai because he was subject to epileptic fits. Naturally the well-trained and ambitious youth was greatly depressed. Some one has said that, in his discouragement, he walked along the banks of the Tiber and its yellow waters quietly told him that in them he might forget his troubles.

With time, however, his health improved and the danger of epileptic attacks passed away. He now determined to enter the Church. He attended lectures at the Collegium Romanum and was ordained priest in 1819. Both his ability and his character were at once perceived, and he was sent to Chile with Monsignor Muzio who was to set in order the affairs of the Church under the new republican form of government. On his return he was put at the head of a large charitable society in Rome. He discharged his duties with a

[1]According to tradition, twenty-five.

motive and an executive power that drew to him the attention of those vitally concerned in the moral and spiritual welfare of the Church. His progress in position and responsibility was rapid. In 1827 Leo XII appointed him to the Archbishopric of Spoleto; in 1831 he was transferred to a like office at Imola. As I have said, he became a cardinal in 1840.

Advancement so rapid, for he was only thirty-five when he was made archbishop and only forty-eight when he was elevated to the cardinalate, must have been caused by positive qualities. And so it was. He was a large man, tall and well proportioned. He had a kindly expression, a very winning smile, and a voice of almost irresistible appeal both in conversation and in the conduct of religious worship. He took excellent care of himself. In days when good people bathed infrequently he took his daily tub, and at a time when beards were popular he shaved every twenty-four hours. He was rather over-careful of his hands, a trait that may have marked a slight touch of effeminacy. As a young man he had been a bold rider. As a young Pope he frequently took his exercise on horseback. He did not care for delicate food. He liked a simple diet and plenty of it, and he preferred water to wine.[2] He loved a picnic and was a jolly companion. He may have

[2]R. de Cesare, *Last Days of Papal Rome*, p. 122.

committed certain irregularities in his youth, but they are neither conspicuous nor were they thought evil by his contemporaries. As priest and bishop he was sympathetic and charitable. It is said that some of his pastoral qualities might match those of a Fénélon. Whenever he had an important question to decide he would ask advice and listen to it, and after praying for direction he would make his decision. He liked books. When he went to Rome in 1846 to attend the conclave which made him Pope he carried with him a number of volumes on the liberal political ideas of the day. Later in life he showed an interest in art and archæology.

He was not a man of conspicuous intellectual ability nor of profound intellectual conviction. As his later career amply proved, his opinion was greatly influenced by the immediate situation in which he found himself. His imagination was meagre. He could not forecast the changing condition of society and regulate his conduct accordingly. In politics, at any rate, difficulty seemed synonymous with error.

Such was the man under whom the Doctrine of Papal Infallibility was passed and under whom the States of the Church were lost.

It is not without significance that in the person of Pius IX the Pope's spiritual power was brought to its highest point at the moment when his temporal power was snatched from his hands. It is interesting to watch the gradual approach of the doctrine of Infallibility during those years in which his civil rule was vanishing.

## I

The doctrine of Papal Infallibility, that is, the doctrine that the Pope can not err when he speaks officially on questions of faith and morals, was implicit in the nature of the Papacy. The claim that our Lord had founded the Church upon Peter and that the Bishop of Rome was his successor; the doctrine that God governed the world with two swords, the State and the Church, and that the sword of the State was inferior to that of the Church; the doctrine that Popes were superior to councils and that no council may have authority unless its conclusions have the Papal sanction—these all lead inevitably to the doctrine that resident within the mind and soul of the Pope there are the mind and soul of God. Pius IX knew that he was a part of this tradition; he was unselfishly and unselfconsciously convinced that he as Pope was endowed with this double personality. Even before the meeting of the Vatican Council in December, 1869, he expressed this feeling in promulgating in 1854 the Doctrine of the Immaculate Conception of the Virgin Mary. Again, this doctrine was implicit in Roman tradition, but Pius made it an explicit part of the faith *motu proprio,* that is, of his own initiative, without the assistance of a council. In 1864 he published another document of singular ecclesiastical importance: in the "Syllabus" he inveighed against the liberal tendencies of the day in religion and politics with all the force that his sacred office supplied. It was but one step from the exercise of this power of initiative to the promulgation of the Doctrine of Infallibility.

Early in the sixties there was talk of a council and of the possible passing of the doctrine. The rumor gathered strength as the decade advanced, and high-minded Romanists quickly formed themselves into three groups: those strongly in favor of it; those who believed in the doctrine but who did not think that the moment had come to declare it;[3] and those who did not believe in it. Of the first were William George Ward and Archbishop Manning, the latter the most persistent of all who for years had prayed and worked for the doctrine. Of the second were Bishop Dupanloup of Orleans, a scholar and pastor of distinction, and John Henry Newman, a spiritual genius. Of the third were Dr. Döllinger, professor of Church His-

[3]Ward, in *W. G. Ward and the Catholic Revival,* p. 244, quotes Newman, "The thing we have to be anxious about is not that there should be no definition, but what the definition will be."

tory at Munich, and Lord Acton, the most fabulously well-informed man in England. The parties ranged, therefore, from those who had long accepted the doctrine and wanted to see it declared at once to those who thought it historically absurd and dreaded its official appearance.

The Pope called a council. It was convened at the Vatican. The first preliminary session was held on December 2, 1869; the second and more formal session on December 8. From the outset it was evident that the Pope was strongly in favor of the doctrine and that he was to urge it with all the force of his personality and his position. The results of certain interviews with the Pope make this abundantly clear. At a critical moment Bishop Ketteler asked for an audience with Pius. It was granted. The Pope received the bishop with the question that revealed the Pope's idea of his office: "Amas Me?" (Lovest thou me?)[4] On another occasion of equal importance Cardinal Guidi ventured to discuss with the Pope the soundness of the doctrine, suggesting that it ran counter to the traditions of the Church. Pius answered "La tradizione son' io" (I am the tradition).[5] And when Cardinal Schwarzenberg expressed to the Pope his doubts about Infallibility, the latter replied, "I, Giovanni Maria Mastai, believe in the

[4]F. K. Nielsen, *The History of the Papacy in the XIX Century*, vol. II, p. 325.
[5]*Ibid.*, 361.

Infallibility."[6] For many years there has been a story to the effect that when the definition was finally passed by the council the Pope said, "In former times, before I was Pope, I believed in the Infallibility; now, however, I feel it."[7]

As the council continued into the summer of 1870 the number of those present decreased. There were various reasons for this singular condition. The delegates had listened to Latin discussions for six months. The summer was approaching and many of the bishops were worn out with their labors. They had been away from their dioceses for a long time and they were anxious to return and set their houses in order. Relations between France and Germany were rapidly nearing the breaking-point. War was imminent. It was but natural that the cardinals of these countries should want to go home. These reasons, however, do not account for the gradual and finally rapid withdrawal of so many. If one may believe the statements of those who kept daily journals and of those whose record of events is preserved in various biographies and histories,[8] one must think that the greater number left Rome either because they were lukewarm about the definition of Infallibility or because they could not be convinced of its his-

[6]*Ibid.,* 323.
[7]Gregorovius, *Roman Journals,* p. 351.
[8]See various Lives of Manning and Gladstone, also de Cesare, *op. cit.*

torical or theological soundness, or because they did not want to remain in the council and resist the obvious wish and will of the Pope, or because of a combination of these reasons. In fact one must come to some such conclusion unless he confines himself exclusively to an abbreviated and thoroughly partisan version of the story.

The event was not altogether uncomplimentary to Pius IX, for even though many would either have postponed the decision until virtually the whole Roman Catholic world was ready for it (this was Newman's very sound position), or would have resisted the definition altogether, they could not bring themselves to oppose the Pope. Personally, he was so winning,[9] and officially he seemed so much more than a man, or even a bishop, that they preferred to withhold their private opinion. There never was a council in which the will of one exercised such mastery. And I know of no council in which opposition to such control faded away so effectively. The council opened with an attendance of 698.[10] On the last ballot 433 voted in favor of the doctrine and two against it.[11] The falling off was tremendous. At that time it was sufficient to make many feel that the decision was not representative. At present,

[9]W. P. Ward, *Life of John Henry, Cardinal Newman,* vol. II, p. 300.

[10]*Catholic Encyclopædia,* see Vatican Council.

[11]W. P. Ward, *op. cit.,* vol. II, pp. 304, 306.

PIUS IX

even though the definition has now been officially valid for sixty years the doubt has not altogether vanished.

On July 18, 1870, the final vote was taken. The circumstances of the fateful decision were impressive. The members of the council were gathered in St. Peter's. It had thundered and lightened all the night before, and it was raining as the bishops went to their work. The Pope said Mass. His voice was firm and clear, although he seemed agitated.

> The Mass was short—and then came those beautiful hymns of the Roman Church sung at intervals, and never sung more effectively. First, the Litany of the Saints was chanted by the Choir taken up by the Fathers and carried as it were out of the Hall until it was lifted on high by the swelling voices of several thousands of persons who clustered around the tomb of St. Peter. So it was with the *Veni Creator*. Apart from the essentially sweet and plaintive character of the music, the body of sound satisfied all one's desires, giving the assurance of something like sincerity and depth of feeling.

The business of the day began. The Secretary read the Dogma. The roll-call and voting followed. The storm now burst with fury.

> And so the placets [ayes] of the Fathers struggled through the storm, while the thun-

der pealed above and the lightning flashed in at every window and down through the dome and every smaller cupola, dividing if not absorbing the attention of the crowd. *Placet,* shouted his eminence or his grace, and a loud clap of thunder followed in response, and then the lightning darted about the baldacchino and every part of the Church and Concilior Hall, as if announcing the response. So it continued for nearly an hour and a half during which time roll was being called, and a more effective scene I never witnessed. Had all the decorators and all the getters-up-of-ceremonies in Rome been employed nothing approaching to the solemn splendor of that storm could have been prepared and never will those who saw it and felt it forget the promulgation of the great Dogma of the Church. The storm was at its height when the result of the voting was taken up to the Pope, and the darkness was so thick that a huge taper was necessarily brought and placed by his side as he read the words—'And we, the sacred Council approving, decree, declare and sanction these things as they have been read.' And again the lightning flickered around the Hall and the thunder pealed. Hands were clapped, handkerchiefs were waved, the crowds without and within St. Peter's shouted 'Long live the Infallible Pope. Long live the triumph of the Catholics.' The Te Deum and the Benedictions however put a stop to it; the entire crowd fell on their knees, as I have never seen a crowd do before

> in St. Peter's. And the Pope blessed them in those clear sweet tones distinguishable among a thousand.[12]

When Pius announced the decision, he said that God was not in the storm, with the evident inference that He was in the still, small voice. Witnesses said that Pius appeared "like a new Moses promulgating the new law." And as a culmination to the impressive ceremony, the Pope, in his friendly, lovely, appealing and well-nigh irresistible manner, asked that those who had opposed the definition might come to a better mind. Thereafter to the loyal Romanist the official definitions of the Pope on matters of morals and faith were to be thought without error.

Such was the spirit of the Vatican Council and such were the circumstances under which Pope Pius IX proclaimed the Dogma of Infallibility.

To add to the dramatic nature of the event which had taken place on July 18 and to account for the speedy adjournment of the council, France declared war on Prussia on July 19.

It was not easy to say what effect the definition would produce. Manning, of course, was so supremely grateful that he was ready to sing his *Nunc Dimittis.* Practically all of the bishops who

[12]Quotations from W. P. Ward, *Life of John Henry, Cardinal Newman,* vol. II, pp. 305, 306.

thought that the definition was either inopportune or wrong quickly yielded to the "Voice of the Church." Newman made his submission, again declaring that his opposition had been only on the ground of the inopportuneness of the definition. "The decree when it came seems to have had the effect of permanently embittering Acton's feelings toward Roman Authority, but he did not, like his friend Döllinger, formally sever his connection with the Church."[13] The nations, however, were disturbed. Even before the council had closed, certain of them had thought of interfering to prevent the decision.[14] And after the definition had been made, they had considered what effect it might have on their subjects' political allegiance. Mr. Gladstone, rather hastily, assumed that the loyal Romanist would thereafter listen to his Pope rather than to his King, and that all the mediæval danger of a divided allegiance might again arise. Newman in a skilful open letter assured the public that such would not be the case. It was a singular coincidence that while Victor Emmanuel was taking from the Pope the last trace of civil authority, certain of the nations of the West should be dreading its practical increase.

The various points of view in regard to the decision open the question as to what shall be the

[13]*Catholic Encyclopædia,* see Acton.
[14]Nielsen, *op. cit.,* vol. II, p. 345.

general attitude toward it. If Manning looked upon it as inherent in the Papal system and as a natural consequence of the Church's development; if Newman, although accepting it as true, would have preferred not to have this "luxury of devotion" officially recognized and therefore turned into another obstacle to further conversions to Romanism; if Acton, apparently, intelligent and devoted Catholic though he was, could never quite reconcile his mind to it; what must one say should be the total outsider's feeling about it? Usually, it is one of complete repudiation and therefore of final dismissal from the mind. The customary reaction against it is somewhat like this: being "mediæval," being "pure superstition," it is not worthy of any serious attention. Those who hold it are benighted; he of whom it is held is merely a survival of the day when demi-gods were thought to be among men and when divinity was supposed to be peculiarly resident in the ruler.

Even the devout Romanist would understand why the outsider should be somewhat bewildered, possibly why he should be utterly unable to conceive of the reasonableness of the doctrine. But will the outsider be contented with any such sympathetic judgment? Will he rest in a purely negative frame of mind in regard to the definition and to those who hold it?

It would seem as if we were confronted with a

problem similar to that of the desire on the part of the Papacy to maintain the Papal States. Whether we can accept the detail of Papal belief or not is not the question. Rather the question is whether we can discover within the doctrine a principle crudely, imperfectly, preposterously put, if you will, and yet possibly a principle in which many of us believe when expressed in some other way. Does not the doctrine become not so much an absurdity to be scrapped as a challenge to our historical imagination and our religious sympathies? Before we can fully appreciate its meaning, must we not take very seriously the fact that after the definition Pius himself was spiritually content and that his feeling was and is shared by hundreds and thousands of high-minded and deeply religious people? Even though we could never express ourselves in a similar way, even though we might much prefer to say that God and man are one when a pure and unselfish purpose is apparent rather than in what may seem a perfect result, must we not recognize that within this belief there is a manifestation of the fundamental longing for the outward and visible union of the divine and the human? Must we not confess that it is a dramatic declaration that God and man must meet not only in the individual but in society, that each in his own way, each in the way that gratifies his mind and his soul, must be able to point to an individual, a group, or a society, and say, "Here I find that man and God are become one in purpose and in action"?

## II

Two reasons underlay the loss of the Papal States. First, they were wretchedly governed. Second, the demand for a united Italy could have but one issue—the absorption of the Patrimony of Peter.

In the Congress of Paris in 1856 Lord Clarendon had openly commented on the manner in which the Papal States were governed. He had said that they were "a scandal to Europe."[15] And so they were, even though other Italian states shared in a like reputation. In days when movements tending toward the education of the people were starting in England, France and Germany, little or nothing was being done by the central and southern Italian kingdoms and the Papacy. At the period when new roads were being made between business centres and when the old roads were being improved, transportation in the Papal States was left in a very primitive condition; and although one of the first of the Italian railways was built with the consent and approval of the Pope, railway development was more rapid in other

[15]Nielsen, *op. cit.,* vol. II, p. 203.

parts of Italy. Brigands by land and smugglers and pirates by sea were common in the heart of Italy and on its coasts long after they had been practically exterminated elsewhere in western Europe. It seemed as if the Papal government were unable to cope with its double function of spiritual and temporal authority. Other governments of the west had long since ceased to employ ecclesiastics in civil offices; Rome's every department was mastered by priests, many of whom were good men, but most of whom were either ignorant or incompetent. Pope Gregory XVI's distrust and dislike of anything "liberal" were a symbol of the actual conditions when Pius IX was elected to the Papacy. It was being rapidly proved that the close union of Church and State, which had, in times gone by, shown itself of incalculable value to both, was an evil rather than a good. The more progressive Romanists perceived the issue and threw in their lot with those who were demanding a separation of the functions.

There were many currents of opinion and action that finally led to the surrender of Rome to Victor Emmanuel. Fairly early in the nineteenth century societies were secretly formed throughout Italy the members of which were sworn to anticlericalism and political freedom. At a somewhat later date their fine, but frequently crudely expressed, ambition was espoused by men of such opposite nature and purpose as Mazzini and Garibaldi. Mazzini was a man of spotless morality and of boundless confidence in human nature. He had but two ideas: God, and a united Italy. Garibaldi, trained on the pampas of South America, a man in love with Italy, picturesquely dressed in red shirt and poncho, fearless, was happy only when he was running some physical risk in a good cause. Each in his own way was to exercise a powerful influence in achieving the national ideal.

Furthermore, Italy as a whole was infected by the democratic spirit that swept over western Europe in the year 1848. As a consequence of this singular burst of democratic feeling, well-established monarchies were likely to become aware of their fundamental insecurity. Sardinia and Piedmont were among the first not only to become conscious of the changing popular demand, but also to take vigorous steps to meet it. From 1848 to 1870 there was a steady desire and an increasingly clear determination in northern Italy to grant the people their share in government and to embody those rights in an ideal which only a united Italy could satisfy. Austria, governed by reactionaries, stood plainly in the pathway over which Italy must pass in the achievement of its purpose. Charles Albert, of the Sardinian royal line, king of Piedmont, knew that Austria must be driven from Lombardy and Venetia if Italy were ever to realize its dream of freedom and of unity. And so he ran the great risk of an attack on a foe vastly his superior. He suffered an overwhelming defeat at Novara. After the battle that secured the control of northern Italy to Austria for another decade, Charles Albert said, "My life has been consecrated to the welfare of Piedmont and of Italy, I perceive now that I am an obstacle to its welfare. To remove this obstacle I have in vain sought throughout this day a bullet; in default of which, abdication remains to me. Gentlemen, I am no longer your king; there is your king, my son Victor."[16]

Patience, diplomacy and preparation were the order of the day from 1848 to 1854. Cavour knew that to succeed Italy must have powerful friends, and so he enlisted the forces of Piedmont on the side of France and England in the Crimean War. The move gave him a standing in the conference of Paris which settled the terms of peace. In payment for its services Piedmont not only was given a hearing, but gained a place among the kingdoms of the West. From now on, Piedmont drew on the sympathy and respect of Austria's enemies. Again a period of waiting and recuperation during which Cavour tried to strengthen the little kingdom in agriculture and finance and in the morale necessary to the task before it.

[16]W. R. Thayer, *The Dawn of Italian Independence,* vol. II, p. 326.

The moment arrived in 1859. In that year Piedmont and France made an alliance the purpose of which was to drive Austria from northern Italy. War was declared. The bloody battles of Magenta and Solferino followed. Austria sued for peace. It surrendered Lombardy; Venetia and the Quadrilateral[17] alone were left to it. It might have retained even less had not Napoleon III, for some unknown reason, possibly the sight of such frightful carnage, possibly dread that a powerful Italy might endanger France, refused to press the war to its obvious conclusion.

Again Cavour accepted the inevitable, using the years of enforced inactivity to stimulate internal prosperity. However, they were not fruitless years, for after Austria's defeat the people of the northern Italian states clamored for union with Sardinia and Piedmont, deposed their kings, and became part of the enlarging kingdom. In 1861 they elected Victor Emmanuel their king. In return, Piedmont surrendered to France Nice and Savoy. And after Austria's defeat by Prussia in 1866 the unfortunate empire, no longer able to retain Venetia, allowed it to become part of the new Italy. Garibaldi was enraged at what he thought the betrayal of Nice, his native land. But Piedmont had an answer in that Savoy was the cradle of her kings. In other words, sacrifice was in order if the larger purpose was to be attained.

[17]Mantua, Peschiera, Verona, and Legnano.

While these events were occurring in the north, a singularly picturesque campaign was taking place in the south. In 1860 Garibaldi had landed in Sicily with his famous Thousand, and had thoroughly conquered the island for the future kingdom. In the same year he had crossed to the mainland, had been joined by an enthusiastic people and had made his way northward as far as the borders of the Papal States. Without having any clearly defined idea of the purpose of his dramatic victories he had prepared half the peninsula for union with the north and for the rapid absorption into the kingdom that was to be. The Papal States alone remained to be conquered.

It is time, therefore, to turn to the centre of Italy and to the Papal policy in regard to the national ideal. Within this drama Pope Pius IX played the title rôle.

Gregory XVI died in 1846. His rule had been not only conservative, but very reactionary. He had frowned on every forward movement in politics and in religion, and it is said he had urged that a conservative be elected as his successor. It was evident, however, that there was a strong liberal party both within and without the College of Cardinals and that Gregory's plans for State and Church would be strongly opposed. Kings, statesmen, and the people watched the conclave with intense interest, knowing that its outcome would determine for many years the policy of the Papal States. For the conclave was to elect not only a spiritual ruler, but apparently for the last time a prince as well.

On their way to the conclave two cardinals were speculating as to the results. One said to the other, "I wonder which one of us will be the next Pope." The other answered, "If the devil inspires the cardinals it will certainly be one of us two, but if the Holy Spirit inspires them, the good Mastai will be Pope." The conclave was very short, lasting only two days. The Holy Spirit inspired the cardinals: Mastai was elected. There was great grief in Austria at the result, but great rejoicing among the people who were looking for better days in Church and State. At last there was a liberal Pope!

The hopes of the people seemed on the point of realization, for Pius was sincerely interested in political reform. He had read widely, if not deeply, on the subjects which were engaging the attention of statesmen and economists, and he reckoned among his friends and well-wishers such men as Charles Albert and Pellegrino Rossi. Furthermore, Pius seems ingenuously to have tried to analyze the political situation and to meet its needs. He at once took steps to improve the methods of finance and jurisprudence, and he made a sweep-

[18]Nielsen, *op. cit.*, vol. II, p. 110.

ing gesture for political peace in granting a general amnesty to all political prisoners. The beginning was promising. The Pope's popularity was at a high point throughout Italy and especially in the Papal States.

His prestige, however, was destined to be short-lived, for the Pope's subjects were bent on two purposes: they wanted the laity to take the place of the clergy in practically all the departments of government and they looked for some kind of Italian national unity. When one considers that since the days of Hildebrand, and before, the clergy had been supreme in the administration of the Papal States,[19] and when one remembers that they had won their supremacy because of their general superiority to the laity; and when one realizes that the Papal States had always had a flavor of internationality rather than of nationality, that they were looked upon not as an Italian, but rather as an unnational, power, by accident resident on Italian soil—one can readily picture the dilemma in which Pius found himself. And one can easily understand that there were two ways of looking at the problem and that honest men might be divided in their opinion. It is to the credit of Pius IX that he could wrench himself sufficiently free from the past to make any concessions at all to the changing present. It may have been that a conserva-

[19]A general statement, subject, of course, to exceptions.

tive, or even a reactionary, Pope could alone be true to the genius of the Papacy.

Pius, almost at once, met the more moderate desires of the people. He may have done so with his whole heart, even though his head may have counselled caution. In the year after his election he permitted the formation of a Roman Council of one hundred members, only four of whom were to be clergy, but many of whom were to be the Pope's personal appointees. He also permitted the formation of a council for the Papal States. Although its candidates were named by the provincial assemblies the Pope made his selection from the nominees, high ecclesiastics were to be in the official positions and matters of unusual weight were to be submitted to the College of Cardinals.[20] Pius had not yet fully gratified the people, but he had gone a long way. He went even farther when in the following year he granted to laymen many of the departments in the Antonelli ministry and when he gave his sanction to a constitution which called for an upper and a lower house. Here, again, however, the Papal personal control was manifest, for the members of the higher chamber were life members, nominated by the Pope. Furthermore, the council could not take cognizance of affairs that were primarily ecclesiastical, and the College of Cardinals was first

[20]*Encyclopædia Britannica.* See Pius (Popes).

to assent to the laws passed by the council. Evidently, for all practical purposes, Pope and cardinals were still supreme.

It is difficult to say how much farther Pius might have gone had not the political issue become involved in the larger problem of Italian independence. While Pius was making certain local concessions to democracy, Charles Albert was vainly trying to drive the Austrians from the north. A wave of sympathy with the attempt of Piedmont seemed for a moment to control the sympathies of the Pope; it looked as if he were about to yield to the popular demand that the Papal armies join with those of Piedmont. On sober thought, however, Pius issued orders that the Papal States should remain neutral. It is not easy rightly to judge his motive. His people were furious; they thought that he was playing them false. They had imagined him one of themselves in the hope for ultimate national unity. On the other hand the angle from which the Pope surveyed the situation was somewhat different. Although he was the temporal head of the Papal States, he was the spiritual head of Austria as well as of Italy. From one point of view, and this had been the point of view of Cardinal Consalvi at an earlier day, the Pope was the temporal ruler of certain territory only that he might with more energy exercise his international spiritual leadership. He was probably quite right in giving the precedence to his international responsibilities, even though his subjects were equally right in insisting that their national feeling should find its natural expression. The Pope's dilemma was due to the anomalous position in which he found himself and out of which twenty years later his own people were to thrust him.

The political tide had turned against Pius. For the rest of his life it never again ran in his favor. It was useless for him to assent to a constant change of ministry, for even certain of his ministers were not in sympathy with him or with his people. He felt that a storm was gathering, and he knew that it had broken when Pellegrino Rossi, his prime minister, a moderate liberal, and a man of vision, was assassinated as he was on his way to open the sessions of the legislature. In the riot that followed, the Pope's secretary was killed and bullets were shot into the Pope's own room.[21] It was well-nigh impossible either to secure a minister who would take Rossi's place or to persuade Pius that any but a nationalist could be found. Wisely he had come to the conclusion that the struggle was over and that flight alone remained to him. While the Duke of Harcourt's carriage was driving up and down before the Quirinal to give the impression that the duke was having an

[21]Nielsen, *op. cit.*, vol. II, p. 162.

audience with the Pope, Pius was putting on the dress of an ordinary priest and escaping by a rear door. At an appointed place Count Spaur was waiting with a carriage. Pope and count drove to Arricia. There the Countess Spaur was waiting with another carriage. She said to the disguised Pope: "Get into my carriage, Doctor, but make haste; I do not like travelling at night." Pius did as he was told and with Count Spaur he was driven to the Neapolitan fortress of Gaëta.[22]

The place which Pius had chosen for his asylum and the friends who gathered themselves about him there were a prophecy of the policy that he was to pursue thereafter. Gaëta was the castle of Ferdinand, king of the two Sicilies, at first an apparent liberal, later a violent reactionary, the sovereign the condition of whose political prisons occasioned Gladstone's terrific invective. Throughout the two years of voluntary confinement at Gaëta Ferdinand was the generous friend and ardent supporter of the Pope. Cardinal Antonelli may stand as another illustration of the kind of influence to which the Pope was subjected. Antonelli was a man of humble extraction, able and utterly unscrupulous. "Tall, robust, well-proportioned; dark-featured, broad-browed, with an 'eagle-beak,' and black penetrating, restless eyes. There was a touch of the Moor in his expression,

[22]*Ibid.*, pp. 164–165.

a hint of the mountain bandit in his free, self-reliant carriage; 'but his heavy jaw, his long teeth, his thick lips betrayed the grossest appetites.' "[23] "Under Gregory XVI he was an orthodox Reactionist; when Pius made liberalism fashionable, he blossomed quickly into a liberal."[24] Although Pius made him a cardinal-deacon Antonelli had a large family of children to whom he left a handsome fortune. Such were the associations gathered about Pius at Gaëta.

Political changes were taking place rapidly at Rome. Relieved of Papal pressure, the nationalists were making progress. Although Pius tried to direct events from afar, he was not permitted to do so. Mazzini was called to Rome and made the head of a triumvirate. A republic was declared. Garibaldi hurried to Rome and offered his services in defence of the city. For nearly two years it seemed as if the Papal government were to be thrown off and a government of the people firmly established in its stead. The nationalists, however, had not sufficiently taken into account the international character of the Papacy. They did not realize that the West in general could not so easily dissociate temporal and spiritual leadership. Even Charles Albert had been opposed to the trend of Roman events. And the governments of the West

[23]W. R. Thayer, *Life and Times of Cavour,* vol. I, p. 179.
[24]*Ibid.,* vol. I, p. 178.

talked of intervention. It was almost unnecessary for Austria to intervene, for at Novara it had successfully checked the national movement in the north. France, which had already stood so dramatically for a democratic form of government, and again was to do so, dispatched an army to save for the Church the Papal States and to restore the Pope. Garibaldi and his enthusiasts for a time bravely defended the city, but in the end superior numbers counted and Rome fell.

Toward the close of his exile at Gaëta, Pius is reported to have said, "I am now anti-constitutional." For twenty years he was to stand against the growing demands not only of his own people, but of all Italy. And he was to be supported in this position not by a powerful native party, but by the sympathy of Austria and by the arms of France. So hard was it for the nations to realize that Church might be separated from State to the advantage of both politics and religion!

After Piedmont's defeat at Novara in 1848, and before its victories at Magenta and Solferino in 1859, the Papal government, free to do virtually as it pleased, became more conservative and reactionary, successfully resisting every movement toward democracy or national unity. The Pope might not only have retained much of his political prestige, but at the same time he might have become nationally necessary and popular had he yielded to the suggestions of such men as Gioberti, Mazzini, and Cavour. The new Italy might have been a federation of states under the Papal presidency. But neither the Pope nor Antonelli would listen to any concession. There was to be no peace with the Italian national ideal.

The fate of the Papal States and of the temporal power of the Popes was to be wrapped up with the fate of France. Naturally the north Italian states under the leadership of Victor Emmanuel did not dare attempt to annex the Papal States while the armies of France were protecting them. Garibaldi, whose services were sometimes of questionable value, could do no more, for the French, at Mentana, had definitely defeated his "Red-Shirts" and had prevented them from joining forces with the insurrectionists in Rome.

The dramatic and long-hoped-for moment arrived, however, in the summer of 1870. The Franco-Prussian War broke out. France withdrew its Roman forces, for every man was needed at home. Victor Emmanuel's government announced to the Powers that his armies would occupy Rome. He asked the Pope to accept his protection instead of continuing as the monarch of the Papal States. The Powers were silent. Pius said that force alone would make him yield. The Italian armies took their position outside the walls of Rome. General Cadorna gave notice that he would attack the city on September 20th unless a peaceful occupation were allowed before that time. Early in the morning of the 20th the Pope celebrated Mass. Afterward he breakfasted with the diplomatists and others who had attended the service. The cannonading of the Italian army was heard throughout the Mass and breakfast. Leaving the foreign ambassadors, Pius withdrew to his private rooms and there the old man played his favorite game of charades, using the word *tremare*[25] for his diversion. When he was convinced that the Italians were serious and when he heard that a breach had been made in the walls near the Porta Pia he ordered the white flag to be raised, and returning to the ambassadors, he said, "Gentlemen, you are witnesses that I yield to the force of violence. Henceforth the Pope is King Victor Emmanuel's prisoner."[26]

The army entered Rome. The Pope was treated with dignity. The people were asked to vote whether they would remain under the old régime, or throw in their lot with Italy. The popular ballot showed that while 1,507 would prefer the Papal government, 133,681 would welcome a united Italy with Rome for its capital and Victor Emmanuel for its King.

The Papal States had fallen. The very close relationship between Church and State, for which

[25]To tremble. [26]Nielsen, *op. cit.,* vol. II, p. 394.

Hildebrand had lived and died, and which had created an internationalism of value to mediæval and possibly to early modern Europe, had apparently finally been dissolved. Nothing was left of the Pope's temporal domain but the properties of the Vatican and the Lateran, and over these he was to have no sovereign rights. From his window he could survey the territory over which he was to remain a monarch by courtesy. Internationalism of the old and useful mediæval type was gone.

In vain Victor Emmanuel tried to reconcile Pius and his ardent supporters to the dramatic change. Pius withdrew from the Quirinal and took up his abode in the Vatican, a defeated and an irreconcilable man. In vain the King offered the Pope ample guarantees of personal freedom from political interference, extra-territorial privileges for the properties of the Vatican and the Lateran, and a generous income to take the place of income lost to the new state. The Pope's person was to be held inviolate and the Pope's immediate properties were to remain uninvaded by the State except with Papal permission. But Pius would never accept a penny of the 3,225,000 lire a year offered him by the national government. He would withdraw into the Vatican; he would consider himself the prisoner of the King; he would not come out until Italy might again recognize him as a prince. He would be a martyr to the theory that a Pope cannot be a free spiritual ruler unless he is subject to no man and unless he is the free monarch of the land on which he lives.

For fifty-eight years Pius and his successors remained within the enclosure of the Vatican; each in this way protesting that Italy was limiting the spiritual power of the Papacy; each with steady persistence refusing to look upon Italian conduct as the faithful wounds of a friend; each standing, as he conceived it, for the principle underlying the conduct of Hildebrand, that the Church must be utterly free from the State. And until very recently it looked as if the Italian State were to continue to make its friendly gestures in vain and as if the Pope's self-imprisonment would endure indefinitely. The disagreement seemed complete and final.

Within the last six or eight years, however, a conviction has gradually possessed the public that the moods of the Quirinal and Vatican were changing and that something was going on that prophesied, in the not distant future, days of peace. And especially has this conviction gained headway since the position of the Fascists under the leadership of Mussolini has become secure. During these years there has been less apparent friction between the two rival powers, and from time to time confiscated properties have been returned to the Church. The traveller in Rome has become aware that a friendly atmosphere was taking the place of the hostile, and that within it new vitality was about to appear. But how few realized that the Pope's fundamental contention was to be granted, that the age-long belief of many people was again to express itself, and that territorial sovereignty was to be thought essential to international spiritual influence!

On February 11, 1929, Cardinal Gasparri, representing Pope Pius XI, and Benito Mussolini, representing King Victor Emmanuel III, met in the Lateran Palace and signed a Financial Convention, a Treaty and a Concordat which later were to be signed by the Pope and the King. Since the Papal and Royal signatures were affixed, and since the new arrangement has become law of Church and State, the world has awakened to the fact that this fundamental mediæval principle will not die and that great numbers of people still cherish the thought that there must be an international religious influence and that it must possibly be superior to any form of State. As one looks back to the days of Pius IX, one cannot help respecting the old man, who, awkwardly, without political imagination, utterly blind to the hopeful social movements gathering headway before his eyes, clung tenaciously to a form of Papal superiority which had become grotesque even to many of the most intelligent friends of the Papacy. It would seem as if one might honor the Pope for his loyalty to the principle, almost forgetting the manner in which his loyalty expressed itself. If at any future day, however far away it may be, there should come into being an international religious influence, unaffected by politics, uncontrolled by limited interests of nations, concerned only with problems of the duty of Christians, the name of Giovanni Maria Mastai Ferretti, Pius IX, will be mentioned with discriminating reverence, for the heart of his contention has been acknowledged by the Kingdom of Italy, and widely acclaimed.

Both Pius IX and his earlier contemporary, Cardinal Consalvi, the man who refused to allow the delicate youth an entrance into the Papal guard, and the one who dared to confront Napoleon with certain principles regarding the relationship between Church and State, the one who, more than a hundred years ago, declared that Papal temporal independence was a condition of political peace and of international spiritual leadership, would be amply satisfied with the spirit, and probably with the letter, of the present agreement between the Papacy and the Kingdom of Italy. How these sentences in the preamble would have comforted their souls! "Assuring to the Holy See in a stable way the condition of fact and of right which guarantees to it absolute independence in fulfillment of its high mission to the world. . . .

To assure absolute visible independence to the Holy See in order to guarantee it indisputable sovereignty also in the international field it is deemed necessary to constitute Vatican City with special dispositions, recognizing its full property rights, with exclusive and absolute power and sovereign jurisdiction over it to the Holy See."[27]

[27]Civis Romanus, *The Pope is King,* pp. 253, 254.

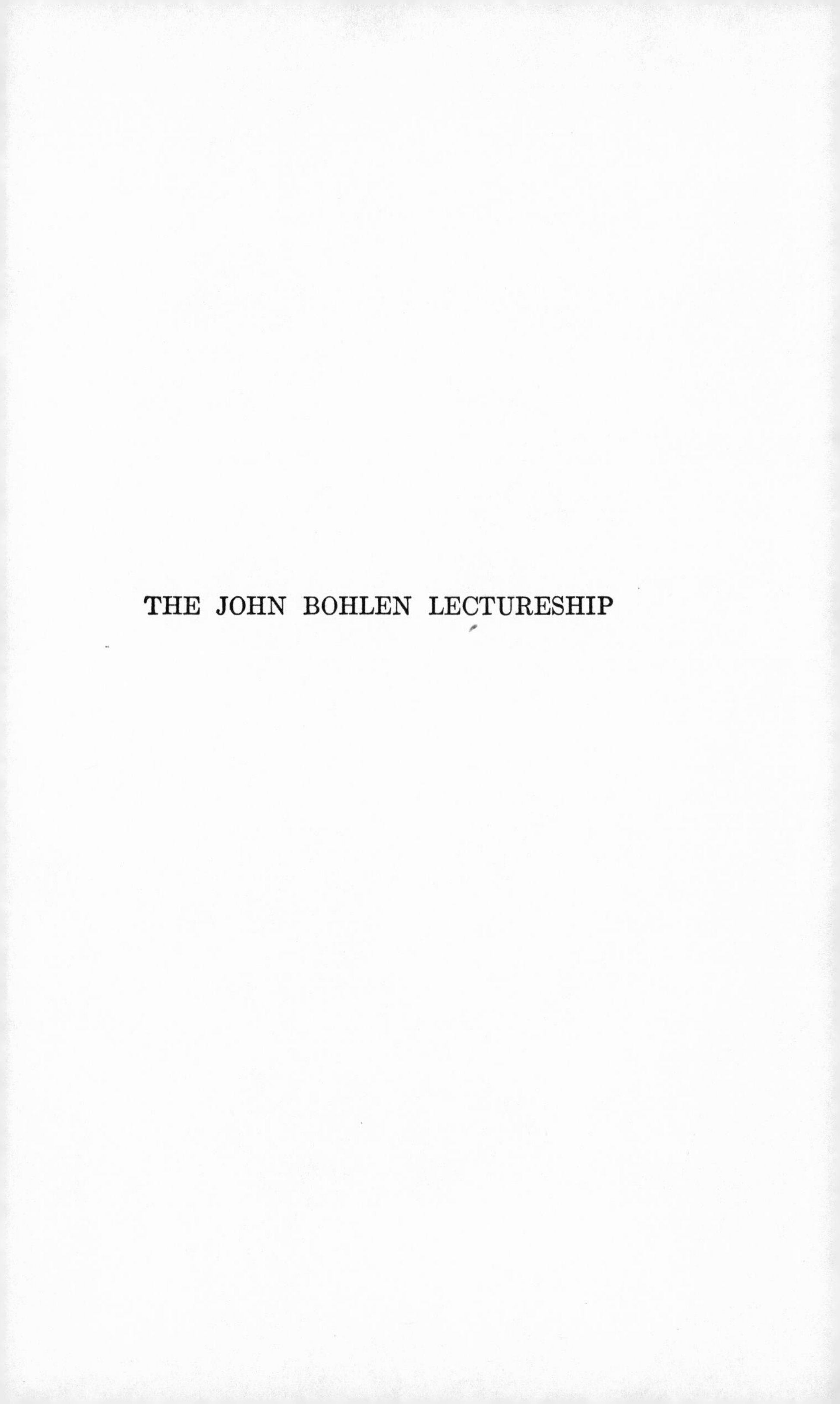

THE JOHN BOHLEN LECTURESHIP

## THE JOHN BOHLEN LECTURESHIP

JOHN BOHLEN, who died in this city on the twenty-sixth day of April, 1874, bequeathed to trustees a fund of One Hundred Thousand Dollars, to be distributed to religious and charitable objects in accordance with the well-known wishes of the testator.

By a deed of trust, executed June 2, 1875, the trustees, under the will of Mr. Bohlen, transferred and paid over to "The Rector, Church Wardens, and Vestrymen of the Church of the Holy Trinity, Philadelphia," in trust, a sum of money for certain designated purposes, out of which fund the sum of Ten Thousand Dollars was set apart for the endowment of The John Bohlen Lectureship, upon the following terms and conditions:

"The money shall be invested in good, substantial, and safe securities, and held in trust for a fund to be called The John Bohlen Lectureship; and the income shall be applied annually to the payment of a qualified person, whether clergyman or layman, for the delivery . . . of two or more lecture sermons. These lectures shall be delivered at such time and place, in the city of Philadelphia, as the persons nominated to appoint the lecturer shall from time to time determine, giving at least six months' notice to the person appointed to deliver the same, when the same may conveniently be done, and in no case selecting the same person as lecturer a second time within a period of five years. The payment shall be made to said lecturer, after the lectures have been printed, and received by the trustees, of all the income for the year derived from said fund. . . .

"The subject of such lectures shall be such as is within the terms set forth in the will of the Rev. John Bampton, for the delivery of what are known as the 'Bampton Lectures' at Oxford, or any other subject distinctively connected with or relating to the Christian Religion.

"The lecturer shall be appointed annually in the month of May, or as soon thereafter as can conveniently be done, by the persons who for the time being shall hold the offices of Bishop of the Protestant Episcopal Church in the Diocese in which is the Church of the Holy Trinity; the Rector of said Church; the Professor of Biblical Learning, the Professor of Systematic Divinity, and the Professor of Ecclesiastical History, in the Divinity School of the Protestant Episcopal Church in Philadelphia.

"In case either of said offices are vacant, the others may nominate the lecturer."

# A LIST OF RECOMMENDED BOOKS


**Athanasius:**

Bright, William. *Lessons from the Lives of Three Great Fathers.* Longmans.

*Cambridge Mediæval History.* Vol. I. Macmillan.

Stanley, Arthur P. *Eastern Church.* Dutton, New York; Dent, London.

**Benedict of Nursia:**

Butler, Edward Cuthbert. *Benedictine Monachism.* Longmans.

*The Dialogues of Saint Gregory, surnamed the Great.* Translated by Edmund L. Gardner. Philips Lee Warner, London.

Montalembert, Charles Forbes René. *The Monks of the West.* Vol. I. Nimmo, London, Kenedy, New York.

Chapman, John. *Saint Benedict and the Sixth Century.* Longmans.

**Hildebrand:**

Wilmot-Buxton, Ethel M. *The Story of Hildebrand, St. Gregory VII.* Burns, Oates, etc., London; Kenedy, New York.

Gregorovius, Ferdinand Adolf. *History of the City of Rome in the Middle Ages.* G. Bell & Sons, London; Macmillan, New York.

*Cambridge Mediæval History.* Vol. V. Macmillan.

**Francis of Assisi:**

*The Legend of St. Francis,* by The Three Companions. Temple Classics. Dent, London; Dutton, New York.

Thomas of Celano. *The Lives of St. Francis of Assisi.* Translated by A. G. Ferrers Howell. Methuen, London; Dutton, New York.

Chesterton, G. K. *St. Francis of Assisi.* Hodder and Stoughton, London; Doran, New York.

Jörgensen, J. *St. Francis of Assisi.* Translated by O.T. O'Conor Sloane. Longmans.

Sabatier, P. *Life of St. Francis of Assisi.* Hodder and Stoughton, London; Scribners, New York.

*St. Francis of Assisi.* Essays in Commemoration. Univ. of London Press.

**Ignatius Loyola:**

Sedgwick, Henry Dwight. *Ignatius Loyola.* Macmillan.

van Dyke, Paul. *Ignatius Loyola.* Scribners.

Longridge, William Hawks. *The Spiritual Exercises of Saint Ignatius Loyola.* Second Edition. R. Scott, London.

**Pius IX:**

Bury, John Bagnell. *History of the Papacy in the Nineteenth Century.* Macmillan.

Butler, Edward Cuthbert. *The Vatican Council.* Longmans.

Romanus, Civis. *The Pope Is King.* Putnam, New York; Benn, London.

Nielson, F. K. *History of the Papacy in the Nineteenth Century.* John Murray, London; Dutton, New York.

INDEX

# INDEX